First World War
and Army of Occupation
War Diary
France, Belgium and Germany

37 DIVISION
112 Infantry Brigade
Essex Regiment
1st Battalion
21 January 1918 - 31 March 1919

WO95/2537/1

The Naval & Military Press Ltd
www.nmarchive.com
Published in association with The National Archives

Published by

The Naval & Military Press Ltd

Unit 10 Ridgewood Industrial Park,

Uckfield, East Sussex,

TN22 5QE England

Tel: +44 (0) 1825 749494

www.naval-military-press.com

www.nmarchive.com

This diary has been reprinted in facsimile from the original. Any imperfections are inevitably reproduced and the quality may fall short of modern type and cartographic standards.

© Crown Copyright
Images reproduced by permission of The National Archives, London, England, 2015.

Contents

Document type	Place/Title	Date From	Date To
Heading	WO95/2537/1		
Heading	37th Division 112th Infy Bde 1st Bn Essex Regt. Feb 1918-Mar 1919. From 29 Div 88 Bde.		
Heading	War Diary Of 1st Battn The Essex Regt. For Month Of February 1918 Mar 19 Volume 36. 3 Div.		
War Diary	Passchendaele	01/02/1918	04/02/1918
War Diary	Wadreques	05/02/1918	14/02/1918
War Diary	Scottish Camp	15/02/1918	15/02/1918
War Diary	Hooge	16/02/1918	20/02/1918
War Diary	Essex House	21/01/1918	26/02/1918
War Diary	Stirling Castle	27/02/1918	28/02/1918
Heading	War Diary Of 1st Essex Regt For March 1918 Volume XXXI Vol 28		
War Diary	Essex House.	01/03/1918	04/03/1918
War Diary	Maida Camp	05/03/1918	09/03/1918
War Diary	Essex Hse	10/03/1918	16/03/1918
War Diary	Stirling Castle	17/03/1918	22/03/1918
War Diary	Maida Camp	24/03/1918	26/03/1918
War Diary	Caestre	27/03/1918	27/03/1918
War Diary	Herrisat	28/03/1918	29/03/1918
War Diary	Thieves	30/03/1918	31/03/1918
Heading	112th Inf. Bde. 37th Div. War Diary 1st Battn. The Essex Regiment. April 1918 Attached: Appendices 1, 2 & 3		
Heading	War Diary Of 1st Essex Regt From 1st April To 30th April 1918 Volume XXXVIII Vol 29		
War Diary	East Of Gommecourt Wood Lic44 Sheet 57 D	01/04/1918	08/04/1918
War Diary	Gommecourt Park	09/04/1918	09/04/1918
War Diary	Bayencourt	10/04/1918	16/04/1918
War Diary	St. Leger	17/04/1918	23/04/1918
War Diary	Essarts.	24/04/1918	30/04/1918
Miscellaneous	Appendices 1, 2 And 3		
Operation(al) Order(s)	Operation Order No. 20 1st Bn. The Essex Regt.	23/04/1918	23/04/1918
Miscellaneous	Defence Scheme for Purple Line and Essarts.	25/04/1918	25/04/1918
Map	B. Rizane 1 Platoon W. Coy.		
Miscellaneous	Essarts Defence Scheme	25/04/1918	25/04/1918
Operation(al) Order(s)	Operation Order No. 23. 1st Battn. The Essex Regiment. Appendix 3	30/04/1918	30/04/1918
Heading	War Diary Of 1st Battalion The Essex Regiment For May, 1918. Volume-39		
War Diary	Essart	01/05/1918	01/05/1918
War Diary	Bucquoy	02/05/1918	12/05/1918
War Diary	Rettemoy Farm	13/05/1918	17/05/1918
War Diary	Louvencourt	18/05/1918	31/05/1918
Heading	War Diary Of 1st Bn. The Essex Regt. From 1st June 1918 To 30th June 1918 Volume 40		
War Diary	Louvencourt	01/06/1918	05/06/1918
War Diary	Briquemesnil	06/06/1918	09/06/1918
War Diary	Flers-Sur-Noye	10/06/1918	13/06/1918
War Diary	St Fuscien	14/06/1918	19/06/1918

War Diary	Rumainsil	20/06/1918	20/06/1918
War Diary	Amplier	21/06/1918	24/06/1918
War Diary	Souastre	25/06/1918	30/06/1918
Operation(al) Order(s)	Operation Order No. A Appendix A.	02/06/1918	02/06/1918
Operation(al) Order(s)	1st Essex Operation Order No. 29 Appendix C.	10/06/1918	10/06/1918
Operation(al) Order(s)	1st Essex Operation Order No. 30. Appendix D.	13/06/1918	13/06/1918
Operation(al) Order(s)	1st Essex Operation Order No. 31. Appendix D.		
Operation(al) Order(s)	1st Essex Operation Order No. 32. Appendix F.	20/06/1918	20/06/1918
Operation(al) Order(s)	1st Essex Operation Order No. 33. Appendix G.	23/06/1918	23/06/1918
Operation(al) Order(s)	Addendum To Operation Order No. 33. Appendix H.		
Heading	War Diary Of 1st Battalion The Essex Regiment For July, 1918. Volume 41		
War Diary	Souastre	01/07/1918	02/07/1918
War Diary	Bucquoy	03/07/1918	10/07/1918
War Diary	Pigeon Wood	11/07/1918	13/07/1918
War Diary	Souastre	14/07/1918	16/07/1918
War Diary	The "Z"	17/07/1918	18/07/1918
War Diary	The "Z" Essarts	19/07/1918	24/07/1918
War Diary	Ablainzevelle	25/07/1918	31/07/1918
Operation(al) Order(s)	1st Essex Operation Order No. 34. Appendix I	01/07/1918	01/07/1918
Miscellaneous	Scheme For Raid In Right Subsector South Of Bucquoy In L.2.d.	13/07/1918	13/07/1918
Operation(al) Order(s)	1st Essex Operation Order No. 37. Appendix 5	18/07/1918	18/07/1918
Miscellaneous	Scheme For Raid North of Bucquoy in F.28.b. &.d.	19/07/1918	19/07/1918
Operation(al) Order(s)	1st Essex Operation Order No. 38	18/07/1918	18/07/1918
Operation(al) Order(s)	1st Essex Operation Order No 39		
Heading	War Diary Of 1st Battn The Essex Regt. For August 1918. Volume 42		
War Diary	Top Trench Ablainvevelle	01/08/1918	04/08/1918
War Diary	The "Z"	04/08/1918	08/08/1918
War Diary	Bucquoy	09/08/1918	19/08/1918
War Diary	Fonquevillers	20/08/1918	20/08/1918
War Diary	Durham Trench	20/08/1918	21/08/1918
War Diary	Halifax Trench	21/08/1918	26/08/1918
War Diary	Pole-Grand	27/08/1918	31/08/1918
Miscellaneous	5th Division Operations On The 23rd August. Attack by the 15th and 95th Infantry Brigade (morning of 23rd)	23/08/1918	23/08/1918
War Diary	Achiet-Le-Grand	01/09/1918	02/09/1918
War Diary	Ebucquiere	03/09/1918	03/09/1918
War Diary	E. of Velu	04/09/1918	06/09/1918
War Diary	Canal N. Of Havrincourt Wood	07/09/1918	09/09/1918
War Diary	Lebucquiere	10/09/1918	10/09/1918
War Diary	East Of Bertincourt	11/09/1918	14/09/1918
War Diary	Trescault Trench	15/09/1918	18/09/1918
War Diary	E. of Velu.	19/09/1918	20/09/1918
War Diary	Warlencourt	21/09/1918	28/09/1918
War Diary	Beugny	29/09/1918	30/09/1918
Heading	War Diary Of 1st Bn The Essex Regt For The Month Of October 1918 Volume 44		
War Diary	Snap Reserve	01/10/1918	04/10/1918
War Diary	La Vacquerie	05/10/1918	06/10/1918
War Diary	Cheneaux Wood	07/10/1918	09/10/1918
War Diary	West Of Caudry	09/10/1918	09/10/1918
War Diary	East Of Bethencourt	10/10/1918	11/10/1918
War Diary	Ligny	12/10/1918	22/10/1918
War Diary	Viesly	23/10/1918	23/10/1918

War Diary	W Of Briastre	23/10/1918	23/10/1918
War Diary	Beaurain	23/10/1918	23/10/1918
War Diary	Neuville	23/10/1918	24/10/1918
War Diary	Salesches	24/10/1918	25/10/1918
War Diary	Ghissignies	26/10/1918	27/10/1918
War Diary	Viterlan	28/10/1918	28/10/1918
War Diary	Beaurain	29/10/1918	31/10/1918
Miscellaneous	1st Battn The Essex Regiment Summary of Operations from 22/10/18 to 27/10/18	22/10/1918	22/10/1918
Heading	War Diary Of 1st Battn. The Essex Regt. For November 1918		
War Diary	Beaurain	01/11/1918	05/11/1918
War Diary	Ghissignies	06/11/1918	11/11/1918
War Diary	Bethencourt	12/11/1918	30/11/1918
Operation(al) Order(s)	1st Essex Regt.-Operation Order No. 71. Appendix I	03/11/1918	03/11/1918
Operation(al) Order(s)	1st. Battn. The Essex Regiment. Amendment To Operation Order No. 71. amendment to Operation order no. 71	03/11/1918	03/11/1918
Operation(al) Order(s)	1st Essex Operation Order No. 72. Appendix II		
Miscellaneous	1st Battn The Essex Regiment. Appendix III	07/11/1918	07/11/1918
Operation(al) Order(s)	1st Essex Operation Order No 75 Appendix IV	30/11/1918	30/11/1918
Heading	War Diary Of 1st Battn The Essex Regt. For The Month Of December 1918 Volume 46		
War Diary	Bethencourt	01/12/1918	01/12/1918
War Diary	Bermerain	02/12/1918	02/12/1918
War Diary	Wargnies Le Grand	03/12/1918	15/12/1918
War Diary	Neuf Mesnil	16/12/1918	17/12/1918
War Diary	Mairieux	18/12/1918	18/12/1918
War Diary	Binche	19/12/1918	19/12/1918
War Diary	Trazegnies	20/12/1918	20/12/1918
War Diary	Ransart	21/12/1918	31/12/1918
Miscellaneous	Return Shewing Decrease In Strength For The Month Of December		
Operation(al) Order(s)	1st Essex Regt-Operation Order No. 75. Appendix II		
Operation(al) Order(s)	1st. Essex Operation Orders No. 76. Appendix III	13/12/1918	13/12/1918
Operation(al) Order(s)	1st Bn The Essex Reg. Operation Order No. 77	14/12/1918	14/12/1918
Operation(al) Order(s)	1st Essex Regt-Operation Order No. 78. Appendix V	16/12/1918	16/12/1918
Operation(al) Order(s)	1st Bn The Essex Reg. Operation Order No. 79. Appendix VI	17/12/1918	17/12/1918
Operation(al) Order(s)	1st Bn The Essex Reg. Operation Order No. 80. Appendix VII	18/12/1918	18/12/1918
Operation(al) Order(s)	1st Bn The Essex Reg. Operation Order No. 81. Appendix VIII	14/12/1918	14/12/1918
Heading	1st Bn The Essex Regt. War Diary Volume XLVII January 1919		
War Diary	Ransart	01/01/1919	31/01/1919
Miscellaneous	Return Shewing Decrease In Strength For The Month Of Jan		
Heading	War Diary Of 1st Bn The Essex Regt. For The Month Of February 1919. Volume 48		
War Diary	Ransart	01/02/1919	28/02/1919
Miscellaneous	Return Shewing Decrease In Strength For The Month Of Feb.		
Miscellaneous	Out Of Irish Free State. 1st Battalion, Essex Regiment, moves from Kinsale to Carrickfergus		

Heading	War Diary Of 1st Battn The Essex Regt For March 1919 Vol 49		
War Diary	Ransart	01/03/1919	10/03/1919
War Diary	Jumet	11/03/1919	31/03/1919
Miscellaneous	Return Shewing Decrease In Strength For The Month Of March 1919	02/04/1919	02/04/1919

W095/25371

37TH DIVISION
112TH INFY BDE

1ST BN ESSEX REGT.
FEB 1918-MAR 1919.

From { 29 DIV
       88 Bde

CONFIDENTIAL

WAR DIARY

OF

1ST BATTN THE ESSEX REGT

FOR MONTH OF

FEBRUARY 1918.

VOLUME 36.

112/37

Army Form C. 2118.

The 1st Bn. The ESSEX REGIMENT.

WAR DIARY
or
INTELLIGENCE SUMMARY
(Erase heading not required.)

Place	Date	Hour	Summary of Events and Information	Remarks and references to Appendices
PASSCHENDAELE	1918 Feby. 1st		The day was very misty and a few clouds of enemy snipers from our the majority of the shots were overhead. We sent out a patrol of 1 N.C.O. and 2 men at 1.55 a.m. until 3 a.m. we found very little information except that the enemy wire was rather weak. Some of the enemy snipers about in front of their lines carrying a red cross flag.	
"	" 2nd		Another very misty day. Enemy Machine Guns were very busy and Battalion Headquarters was subject to heavy shelling at 3.15 a.m. No. 4 Post held by "Z" Company (left Company) were raided by 1 Officer and 25 Other ranks of the enemy at 10.15 p.m. but were driven off leaving no rifles and one phomen. A carrying party of No. 5 Platoon "W" Company the 1st HAMPSHIRE REGT. dumped their ration and took up their position in the post and helped to drive the raiders off. A letter was sent to the C.O. of the 1st Bn. HAMPSHIRE REGT thanking them for their help.	

WAR DIARY
INTELLIGENCE SUMMARY

Army Form C. 2118.

Place	Date	Hour	Summary of Events and Information	Remarks and references to Appendices
PASSCHENDAELE	July 3rd		The day was showery and enemy aircraft were fairly active over our lines but were driven off by our Lewis Guns. The enemy shelled a good deal especially the tracks leading to front line.	
			At 11:15 p.m. 16 guides proceeded from Battalion H.Q. to the SOMME crossing Station (ST JEAN – WEILTJE ROAD) to meet the 1st Bn. BORDER REGT.	
			At 5:45 p.m. the 1st BORDER REGT arrived and were taken by guides to front line where they relieved us. Relief completed at 1:15 a.m.	
	4th		At 1:45 a.m. the first train load of the Battalion left WEILTJE STATION for BRANDHOEK, the second train left at 3:30 a.m. arriving at BRANDHOEK at 5:45 a.m., then marching to WARRINGTON CAMP.	
			At 2:30 p.m. the Battalion marched to VLAMATINGHE STATION. This is our last day with the 29th DIVISION as we are to be transferred to the 37th and everybody feels it very much as it was indeed a fine division. GEN'L. FREYBURG V.C. D.S.O. and the commanding officers of the other regiments in our old Brigade came to the Station to bid us farewell. Our drums and three of the WORCESTER, HAMPSHIRE and NEWFOUNDLAND REGTS. played while we	

Army Form C. 2118.

WAR DIARY
INTELLIGENCE SUMMARY.
(Erase heading not required.)

Instructions regarding War Diaries and Intelligence Summaries are contained in F. S. Regs., Part II. and the Staff Manual respectively. Title pages will be prepared in manuscript.

Place	Date	Hour	Summary of Events and Information	Remarks and references to Appendices
	Sct 4th		(Continued) were entraining and GENL. de LISLE inspected the Battalion before they left. At 4 pm we left for EBBLINGHEM arriving at 7 pm and then marched to WADREQUES to our billets.	
WADREQUES	5th		Battalion Resting. The Billets are good.	
"	6th		Battalion Resting	
"	7th		Battalion parade for inspection by the Commanding Officer prior to inspection by the Brigadier of our new Brigade.	
"	8th		Battalion inspected by Brigadier of 112th Bde. It rained slightly during the day.	
"	9th		Battalion Training, under Company arrangements	
"	10th		Weather unsettled. Battalion church parade.	
"	11th		Weather dull. Training. At 4.15 pm a draft of 7 4 officers and 97 other Ranks arrived from the 13th BN. ESSEX REGT who have been dis-bounced.	
"	12th		Battalion training. Weather dull but brightened towards the afternoon. At 4 pm a draft of 55 other ranks arrived from 13th BN. ESSEX REGT.	
"	13th		Rained all day. The 2nd in Command left Battalion Headquarters to see back area.	

WAR DIARY
INTELLIGENCE SUMMARY.
(Erase heading not required.)

Army Form C. 2118.

Place	Date	Hour	Summary of Events and Information	Remarks and references to Appendices
VARDREQUES	Set 14th		General training of the Battalion carried out. Baths were arranged for the draft from the 13th Bn ESSEX REGT. Received orders for moving Battalion	
Scottish Camp	" 15th		Battalion paraded at 7.30am and marched to EBBLINGHEM, went by train to DICKEBUSCH and marched to SCOTTISH CAMP. We took on the camp from a Battalion of the SOMERSET LIGHT INFANTRY at	
		2 pm.	Brigade Headquarters at LA CLYTTE.	
HOOGE	" 16th		Battalion went into Brigade Support at HOOGE CRATER on the MENIN ROAD. "W" Company at JARGON TUNNELS. "X" Company CLAPHAM JUNCTION and "Y" and "Z" at JACKDAW TUNNELS. The night was very quiet.	
"	" 17th		Day passed quietly. Dispositions rendered to Brigade. Storming tactics carried in front line at 4.30 pm but the alarm proved false.	
"	" 18th		Artillery S.O.S Barrage was put down at 3.20 am. A great deal of Salvage was obtained during the day. The tunnels were also drained and cleaned. Day passed quietly.	
"	" 19th		More salvage collected, also two latrines built and extra beds put up in the tunnels.	

WAR DIARY

INTELLIGENCE SUMMARY.

(Erase heading not required.)

Army Form C. 2118.

Place	Date	Hour	Summary of Events and Information	Remarks and references to Appendices
Hooge	Feb. 20th		The day passed very quietly indeed and we provided working parties all day and all night salvage.	
ESSEX HOUSE	" 21st		The Battalion went into the line relieving the 8th Bn. LINCOLNSHIRE REGIMENT at ESSEX HOUSE. Relief complete at about 7.30 pm	
"	" 22nd		The day was quiet dispositions were reported to Brigade and three patrols went out during the night	
"	" 23rd		The enemy Machine Guns were more active than usual today. Three patrols went out during the night.	
"	" 24th		We evacuated our front posts for the day to allow the Artillery to shell the enemys front line. Nearly 12 direct hits were obtained on LEWIS HOUSE – LEWIS HOUSE Trench Morters were quiet during the evening but Machine Guns were very active.	
"	" 25th		The day passed quietly. The enemys Trench Morters and Machine Guns were more active than usual.	
"	" 26th		A gas barrage was put down by the enemy in rear from position (through DUMBARTON WOOD) at about 12.15 am 27.2.18. The Battalion was relieved by the	

Army Form C. 2118.

WAR DIARY
INTELLIGENCE SUMMARY.
(Erase heading not required.)

Place	Date	Hour	Summary of Events and Information	Remarks and references to Appendices
ESSEX HOUSE	Sept. 26		(continued) 6th Bn. BEDFORDSHIRE REGT. and we went into Brigade Support at STIRLING CASTLE	
STIRLING CASTLE	Sept. 27		Corps front. The day passed quietly. Our artillery registered during the afternoon on the enemy's line.	
"	" 28		The weather was fine. Our Artillery put down a barrage on the enemy's line at 3am lasting for three quarters of an hour and again at 5.30am lasting a quarter of an hour otherwise everything has been very quiet.	

H Knight
LT.-COLONEL
COMDG. 1st BN. THE ESSEX REGT.

Frank A. Brown Lieut
I.O. 1st Bn ESSEX RGT.

112/37

Vol 28

28.N.

WAR DIARY
of
1st ESSEX REGT
for
MARCH 1918

VOLUME XXI

1st ESSEX REGT.

WAR DIARY
or
INTELLIGENCE SUMMARY
(Erase heading not required.)

Army Form C. 2118.

Instructions regarding War Diaries and Intelligence Summaries are contained in F.S. Regs., Part II. and the Staff Manual respectively. Title pages will be prepared in manuscript.

Place	Date	Hour	Summary of Events and Information	Remarks and references to Appendices
ESSEX HOUSE	MARCH 1.		Rained during day. At 4.15 am. Bn. Artillery put down a Barrage on enemy's line for 1/4 hour. At 11 am. we used our K.T. shells with gas shells. Generally the day was quiet. 3.05 on my left at 10.15 pm	
	2.		Day generally dull. Snowed in afternoon. Day very quiet.	
	3.		Day chill & rather cold. Generally quiet.	
	4.		Day quiet. Rained. Were relieved by 6th BEDFORDS. Relief complete at 12.45 am. Coys marched to MAIDA CAMP for 6 days rest.	
MAIDA CAMP	5.		Bn. resting. Baths were arranged for Coys.	
	6.		Bn. paraded for inspection by C.O. Each Coy called for to Centre for a rest. A party of 4 Officers and 60 ORs were selected. Each Cooks just in charge of rest.	
	7/9.		Training under Coy arrangement.	
	10.		At 6 pm Bn moved off from MAIDA CAMP to Front Line to relieve 13th R.F.s. Relief completed 11-30 pm	
ESSEX HSE	11.		Misty morning. 2-30 pm direct hit on W. Coy HQrs 2 Officers (Lt Crampton & Lazar B.J.) C.S.M. & 3 OR wounded. Gas in PERTH AVENUE. Artillere Shoot at 7.15 pm. (30 minutes) & 4.45 am (20 minutes)	
	12.		Quiet day. 3 Patrols out during night. Patrol ordered coming out. 3 Casualties 6 ORs.	
	13.		Intermittent artillery all day. Arty Shoot on enemy defences at 9.20 am for 25 minutes	
	14.		Issued at our cables at 9.20 pm unsuccessful raid on enemy trenches in vicinity of J22.a.3.2. (ZILLEBEKE Sheet 28 N.W.) Casualties. Lt Hopewood, & 2 ORs wounded. 1 OR missing. 4.20 am. Heavy hostile barrage for 35 minutes.	
			Several casualties at Bn. HQ. & Lt. Cotham wounded.	

1st ESSEX REGT.

WAR DIARY
or
INTELLIGENCE SUMMARY
(Erase heading not required.)

Army Form C. 2118.

Place	Date	Hour	Summary of Events and Information	Remarks and references to Appendices
ESSEX HSE.	MARCH 15.		Hostile arty active until 10 a.m., then quietened until 3.30 p.m. New gas used "Blue Cross".	
	16.		Sham fight. Relieved by 6th BEDFORDS. Bn. went to STIRLING CASTLE. Cpl. Goora severely wounded in leg.	
STIRLING CASTLE	17.		Aeroplane practice at night. Heavy gas bombardment.	
	18/22		Ensail gut. Relieved by 6th BEDFORDS & went to MAIDA CAMP.	
MAIDA CAMP	24/26		MAIDA CAMP. Bn. training with Bde. at maneuvers.	
CAESTRE	27.		Entrained & went to CAESTRE. Arrived between 5 & 6 p.m.	
HERRISAT	28.		Left CAESTRE & marched to MONDICOURT. From there Bn. marched to HERRISAT arriving there at 11 p.m. on 29th. 37th Bde. was transferred to 4th CORPS. 3rd ARMY.	
THIEVES	30.		Balln. ent. 150 O.R. embussed to THIEVES. arriving 2 p.m. 150 men marched arriving at 6 p.m. transferred to the 63rd. 3rd ARMY.	
THIEVES	31.		Balln. entrained at THIEVES to FONQUEVILLERS, and relieved 1/6th Bde., No. relieved 8th W. YORKS + 3 Coys of 2/4 WEST RIDINGS. Relief compl. at 4 am. 1/4/18.	

112th Inf.Bde.
37th Div.

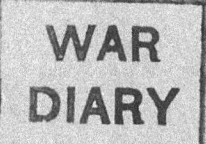

1st BATTN. THE ESSEX REGIMENT.

A P R I L

1 9 1 8

Attached:

Appendices 1, 2 & 3.

CONFIDENTIAL

WAR DIARY

OF

1ST ESSEX REGT.

FROM 1ST APRIL TO 30TH APRIL

1918

VOLUME XXXVIII

Army Form C. 2118.

WAR DIARY
INTELLIGENCE SUMMARY.
(Erase heading not required.)

Instructions regarding War Diaries and Intelligence Summaries are contained in F. S. Regs., Part II. and the Staff Manual respectively. Title pages will be prepared in manuscript.

Place	Date	Hour	Summary of Events and Information	Remarks and references to Appendices
East of GOMMECOURT wood. L1.C.4.4. Sht 57D	1st	11pm	Relieved 1st Division 5th Brigade and 3 Companies 2/4th West Ridings in a front of about 1300 yards from centre of ROSSIGNOL wood to L2.C.2.2.	Nil.
	2nd		Heavy intermittent Shelling. Lt. R. BAKFORD wounded.	Nil.
	3rd	9.30pm 10.0am	4 prisoners of 8th R.I.R. 1st Guard Res. Division captured in daylight raid.	Nil
	4th		2 Enemy. No active Participation	Nil
	5th			
	6th		Heavy intermittent Shelling. Trenches heavy, but few heavy than which continue quiet	Nil
			all were to prepare for attack on Trench feb.	Nil.
	7th 8th		Raining again fell.	Nil.
FONCHECOURT PARK	9th	11.55	Relieved by 1st Middlesex & marched to FONCHECOURT PARK, reaching War front at	Nil
BAYENCOURT	10th	6pm 4.0 am.	Lieut S. PRESTON killed by G.S.W. March from FONCHECOURT PARK, but halted to BAYENCOURT awaiting orders at 8 pm, not known attacked.	Nil
	11th		Rested.	Nil.
	12th		Lieut Hon. I.M Chaplin late on command of trenches from Lt/Col Sir George Steplin. Batt Dio. Lt/Col. J Mafeil DSO 2 in command appointed temporary Composite Batterin	Nil

WAR DIARY
INTELLIGENCE SUMMARY.
(Erase heading not required.)

Army Form C. 2118.

Instructions regarding War Diaries and Intelligence Summaries are contained in F. S. Regs., Part II. and the Staff Manual respectively. Title pages will be prepared in manuscript.

Place	Date	Hour	Summary of Events and Information	Remarks and references to Appendices
BIENVILLERS	13	7·0 p	Marched GOMMECOURT to BIENVILLERS. Training. Defence of POZIÈRES line. Coy A	Appendix I
			MONCHECOURT.	
	14(?)		Working parties to trenches. Afternoon	nca.
	15		Working parties in the trenches. GOMMECOURT heavy shelling.	nca.
	16		2nd Lt R. CURZON HOPE wounded.	nca.
ST LEGER	17	11·0 a	Relieved by 1/7 Lancashire Fusiliers. Marched to ST LEGER to AUTHIE	nca.
			Arriving at 4·0 a.m.	nca.
	18		Battalion training.	nca.
	19		Company training. Lt Col A.R.C. SANDERS CMG DSO took over command 1st	nca.
			Battalion	
	20		Work in Red line defences.	nca.
	21		Company training. Red troops his removed	nca.
	22		Practice manning Red line.	nca.
	23		Company training	nca.
ESSARTS	24	6 p	Marched ESSARTS. Relieving 2/7 Duke Wellington Regt. Relief complete	Appendix I
			11.20 p.m.	nca.

Army Form C. 2118.

WAR DIARY
INTELLIGENCE SUMMARY.
(Erase heading not required.)

Instructions regarding War Diaries and Intelligence
Summaries are contained in F. S. Regs., Part II.
and the Staff Manual respectively. Title pages
will be prepared in manuscript.

Place	Date	Hour	Summary of Events and Information	Remarks and references to Appendices
Essars	25		Work on defence thbnys.	NA 2
	26		Work on defence	NCA
	27		Work on defence	NCA
	28		Work on defence	NCA
	29		Work on defences	NCA
	30		Work on defences. 1 O.R casualty owing to enemy shelling	NCA
			Orders received to relieve front line Buckuoy sector	3

APPENDICES

1, 2 and 3.

Operation Order No 20.
1st/13th The Essex Regt.

Copy No 2
23.4.18

Reference 1:20,000.
France 57. D.N.E.

INFORMATION 1. (a) The 37th Division is relieving the 62nd Division.
(b) The 112th Infantry Brigade will relieve the 186th Infantry Brigade in Divisional Reserve on the night 24/25 April

INTENTION 2. The 1st Essex Regt will relieve the 2/7th Duke of Wellington's Regt at ESSARTS

DETAIL 3. (a) Route.
COUIN – SOUASTRE – FONCQUEVILLERS – LA BRAYELLE Road.

(b) Starting Point. – Road Junction T.12 Central at Bde Headquarters.

(c) TIME. – Head of main body will pass Starting point at 6 pm.

(d) Order of March. H.Q Company X, Y, Z, W, Coys (marching in file) 1st Line Transport (up to SOUASTRE) After leaving SOUASTRE, Coys will march independently by platoons at 200 yds interval.
DRESS. – Fighting Order.

(e) Guides will meet companies at road junction East of FONCQUEVILLERS E 22 C.O.1.

(f) Order of Relief.
    X Coy 1st Essex will relieve B Coy 2/7 D. of W.
    Y " " " " " C " " "
    Z " " " " " D " " "
    W " " " " " A " " "

(g) The band will play the battalion to SOUASTRE.

(h) Officers' Valises & mess boxes will be stacked at dump by 5 pm.

(i) The following Officers with other details will join the Composite Bn. at AUTHIE.
    Major R. C. Carthew M.C.
    Capt. S. J. Griggs.
    Lieut. C. Wark.
      " A. B. Neal.
      " G. A. Fortescue
    2/Lieut W. H. Digby.
Parade 4.15 pm outside Orderly Room

(j) The Transport & Quartermasters Stores with the band, Company Administrative Staffs, 2/Lieut. A. P. H. Davison and Orderly Room Staff will move to SOUASTRE. The Quartermaster will arrange a small advance party & notify time of parade for these details

(k) Billets will be cleared & ready for inspection at 5 pm

(l) Water bottles will be filled.

(m). Lewis Guns will be carried on Lewis Gun limbers and will be loaded by 5.30 pm.
Companies will be notified as to where the Lewis Guns will be unloaded.

Reports 4: Companies will report relief complete by the code words "DRUMS".

Acknowledge 5.

P. H. Sharp.
Captain
Adj 1/Essex Regt.

Issued by Orderly at 8.15 p.m.

DEFENCE SCHEME
FOR
PURPLE LINE AND ESSARTS.

1. The Brigade in reserve is responsible for manning the 1st & 2nd PURPLE LINE which must be held at all costs.

2. The 1st Battn. The Essex Regt will man the left sub sector from about F.25.a.1.7 (inclusive) to F.20.a.1.8, where the divisional boundary runs with 32nd Division.

3. 'X' Company will hold from F.25.a.1.7 to F.25.a.7.9 (BRADFORD TRENCH) & BRIDLINGTON POST (E.24.d.3.4). Company HQrs KITE COPSE.

   'W' Company will hold from F.19.c.3.2 to F.19.c.9.7 and YORK POST (F.19.c.6.4). Company HQrs E.24.b.7.1.

   'Y' Company will hold from F.19.c.9.7 to F.20.a.1.8 (CONEY STREET) and DICK HUDSON'S POST (F.19.b.3.7.) Company HQrs F.19.a.4.0.

   'Z' Company (in support) will hold the second PURPLE LINE with posts at HULL (E.24.d.3.7.) and HALIFAX (F.19.a.5.6). ~~Company HQrs E.24.~~ and HELL (E.24.b.0.1) Company HQrs E.24.d.8.8.

4. BATTALION HEADQUARTERS at E.24.d.8.8.

5. AID POST at 'W' Coys HQ.

6. On the alarm being given by the code word "JUMP", or if warning is received that an attack is imminent, all battle positions will be manned.

25.4.18.

[signature]
LT.-COLONEL,
COMDG. 1st BN. THE ESSEX REGT.

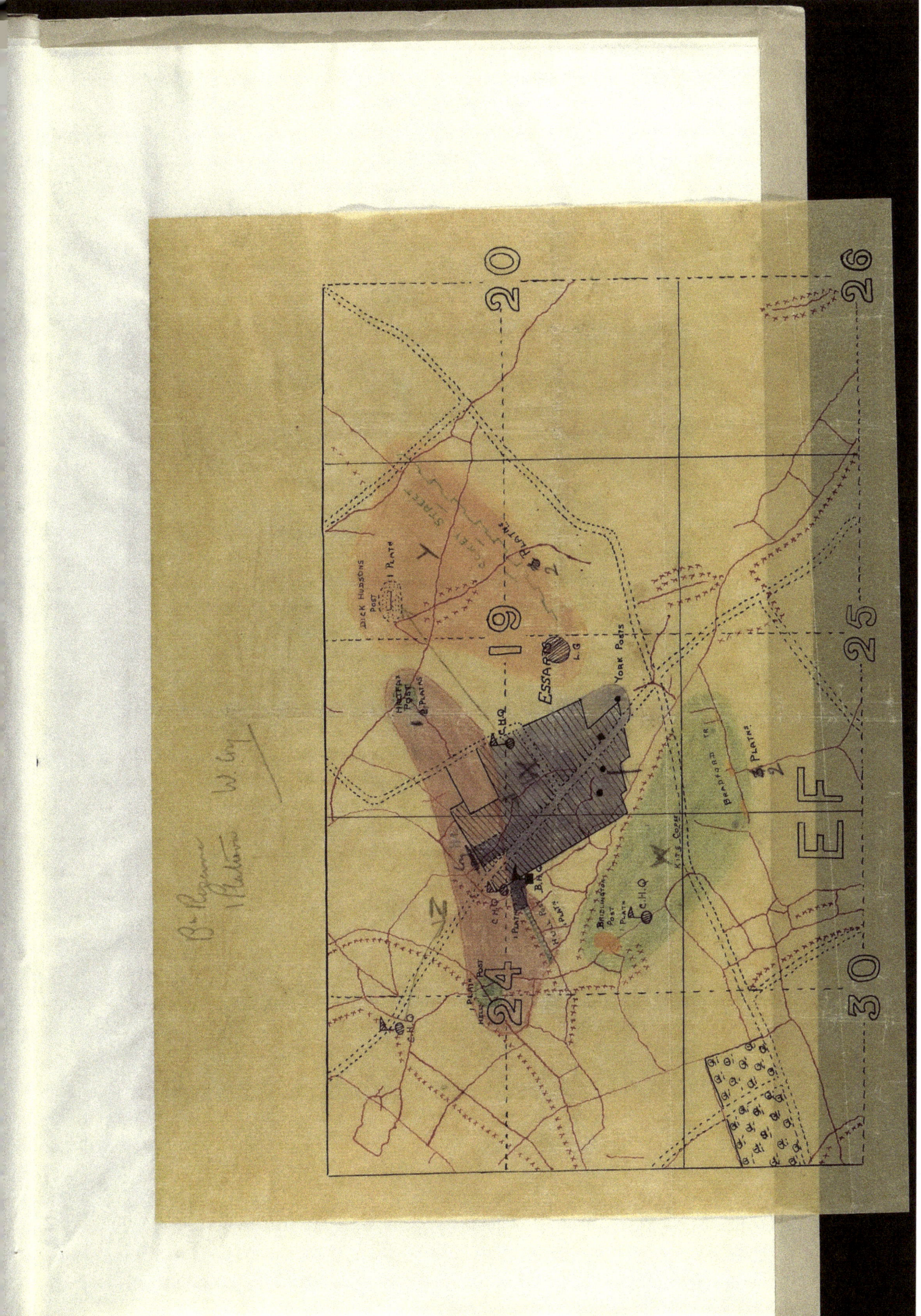

ESSARTS DEFENCE SCHEME

Distribution in detail.
X Coy.
  BRADFORD TRENCH. { one platoon
          { one L.G. section
  BRIDLINGTON POST { 2 Sections
          { 2 L.G. Sections.

Y Coy. CONEY TRENCH Two platoons
  DICK HUDSON'S POST. One platoon
  1 L.G. in reserve Coy HQ

Z Coy. HULL POST. one platoon.
  HELL POST one L.G. section.
  HALIFAX POST one platoon
  One L.G. for AA work

W Coy. YORK POSTS. Three platoons.
  one L.G. reserve Coy HQ

25/4/18

A.R. Sanders
Tpl.
Cmdg Essarts Regt

OPERATION ORDER No. 23. Appendix
1st BATTN. THE ESSEX REGIMENT   3.

REF: MAP.   Copy No. 10
5.0. 1/40,000.   30.4.16.

INFORMATION. 1. The 112th Infantry Bde. will relieve
              the 161st Infantry Bde. in the Right
              Section of the Divisional Area on
              the night of 2nd/3rd May.
           2. Units of the 161st Infantry Bde. are
              withdrawing on relief to Brandon
              vacated by this unit & the relieving
              units of this Brigade.

INTENTION. 3. The 1st Essex Regt. will relieve the
              4th Battn. Somerset Light Infantry
              in the Right Sub-section.

DETAIL.   4. (a) Order of March.
              H.Q. Coy. relieving H.Q. Coy. 4th S.L.I.
  (FRONT LINE – X Coy. relieving B Coy. (Left)
  (FRONT LINE – Z Coy.   "   D Coy. (Right)
   SUPPORT   – W Coy.   "   A Coy.
   RESERVE   – Y Coy.   "   C Coy.
              (b) Starting Point Cross roads immediately
              SOUTH-EAST of ESSARTS. C.E.19.c.8.d.

              (c) Time – 10 p.m.

(d) Platoons will march at 200x
interval.

(e) Guides will meet the Battalion at
junction of road & railway at
F.26.c.2.7.

(f) Advance party of 1 Officer & 1 N.C.O.
per Front Line Coy. will report to
B.H.Q. 8th S.L.I. at F.26.a.3.2. at
3 pm to-day. 1 Officer & 1 N.C.O.
per Support, Reserve & Headquarters
Coy. will report to B.H.Q. 8th S.L.I.
at 3 pm 1st May.

1 Officer & 4 N.C.O.s per Coy. and
1 N.C.O. per H.Q. Coy. 8th S.L.I. will
report to their headquarters at
3 pm 1st May.

(g) Trench Stores Defence Scheme &c.
will be taken over from Units being
relieved & receipts given. Lists
in duplicate to reach B.H.Q.
by 12 noon 2nd May.

(h) Dispositions & details of flank
liaison accompanied by sketch
if possible will reach B.H.Q. by
8 am 2nd May.

(4) Rations will be delivered as usual at 3.30 p.m. on 1st May. All water bottles will be filled before going into the line and all dixies will be returned by transport on that day. Coy. cooks will accompany transport.

(5) All dug-outs will be left clean.

REPORTS 4. Completion of relief will be wired to B.H.Q. by code word "SWANK".

ACKNOWLEDGE 5.

                                          [signature]
Issued by order at: Capt. & Adj.
                                    1st Bn. The Essex Regt.

CONFIDENTIAL.

WAR DIARY

OF

1ST BATTALION THE ESSEX REGIMENT

FOR

MAY, 1918.

———

VOLUME - 39.

———

Army Form C. 2118.

WAR DIARY
or
INTELLIGENCE SUMMARY.
(Erase heading not required.)

Instructions regarding War Diaries and Intelligence Summaries are contained in F. S. Regs., Part II. and the Staff Manual respectively. Title pages will be prepared in manuscript.

Place	Date	Hour	Summary of Events and Information	Remarks and references to Appendices
	MAY			
ESSART	1	9.30 p.m.	Battn. marched to BUCQUOY and relieved 8th Battn. Somerset Light Infantry in front line. Relief complete at 12 m.n.	Appendix
BUCQUOY	2	—	Day passed quietly. Work on trench shelters and improvement of positions. Casualties 2 O.R. wounded.	
	3	—	Wiring of main line commenced and shelters improved.	
	4	11 a.m.	Heavy hostile shelling. Casualties 2 O.R. wounded by snipers.	
	5	11 p.m.	W and Y Coys relieved in front line by W and Y Coys respectively. Casualties 1 O.R. killed and 1 O.R. wounded.	
	6	—	Day passed quietly	
	7	—		
	8	2 p.m.	We advanced one of our posts in cooperation with the 13th Battn. Rifle Bde attacking on our left. Our positions were heavily shelled and we suffered as casualties Lt J A Howard died of wounds 2/Lt A J Pearson wounded 5 O.R. killed and 7 O.R. wounded.	
	9	—	Slight hostile shelling of our position at odd periods during the day. Front line Coys relieved.	

Army Form C. 2118.

WAR DIARY
or
INTELLIGENCE SUMMARY.
(Erase heading not required.)

Instructions regarding War Diaries and Intelligence Summaries are contained in F.S. Regs., Part II. and the Staff Manual respectively. Title pages will be prepared in manuscript.

Place	Date	Hour	Summary of Events and Information	Remarks and references to Appendices
	MAY			
BUCQUOY	10	—	Day passed quietly	NCR
"	11		" Casualties, 3 O.R. wounded.	NCR
"	12	9.30 p.m.	The batt. was relieved by 13th Batt. Royal Fusiliers and moved into Brigade reserve at RETTEMOY FARM. Casualties 19 O.R. wounded by gas shelling in FONCQUEVILLERS	Appendix No II NCR
RETTEMOY FARM	13		Day passed quietly Casualties 10 O.R. killed	NCR
"	14	6.30 p.m.	Rettemoy Farm and vicinity heavily shelled. Casualties: Capt A.W. NEW accidently wounded	NCR
	15		Hostile artillery less active. Casualties 4 O.R. gassed.	NCR
	16		Day passed quietly. Casualties 2 O.R. wounded.	NCR
	17	11.30 p.m.	Batt. relieved by 8th Batt. West Yorkshire Regt. marched to Couin and thence proceeded by train to LOUVENCOURT arriving 5 a.m. 18/5/18.	NCR Appendix No III
LOUVENCOURT	18		Baths	NCR
	19		Company training	NCR
	20		Company training	NCR
	21		Range practice and company training	NCR
	22 23 24		Digging on Purple Line at SAILLY-au-BOIS.	NCR

WAR DIARY
or
INTELLIGENCE SUMMARY.

(Erase heading not required.)

Army Form C. 2118.

Place	Date	Hour	Summary of Events and Information	Remarks and references to Appendices
	MAY			
LOUVENCOURT	25	—	Baths	n.a.
"	26	10 a.m.	Church parade. Football match versus 26th Regt French Infantry. Result 5 goals to 2 in our favour	n.a.
	27		Training by Companies	n.a.
	28		Range practices and training	n.a.
	29		Battn parade for ceremonial drill	n.a.
	30	10 a.m.	Inspection by G.O.C. Brigade	n.a.
		10.30 p.m.	Red line defences manned	n.a.
	31	9 a.m.	Battn Field Day.	n.a.

CONFIDENTIAL

WAR DIARY

OF

1ST. BN. THE ESSEX REGT.

From 1st. June 1918 to 30th. June 1918

VOLUME 40

Army Form C. 2118.

WAR DIARY
or
INTELLIGENCE SUMMARY.
(Erase heading not required.)

Instructions regarding War Diaries and Intelligence Summaries are contained in F. S. Regs., Part II. and the Staff Manual respectively. Title pages will be prepared in manuscript.

Place	Date	Hour	Summary of Events and Information	Remarks and references to Appendices
	JUNE			
LOUVENCOURT	1		Range practice	NCA
"	2	10 a.m	Church Parade	NCA
"	3		Brigade Field day	NCA Appendix A.
"	4		Baths and Company training. Transport moves at 8 p.m.	NCA
"	5		Training programme cancelled, awaiting orders to move. Battn. embussed at 11.30 p.m. and arrived at BRIQUEMESNIL at 5 a.m. 6/6/18	NCA Appendix B.
BRIQUEMESNIL	6	8 p.m	Battn Concert	NCA
"	7	9.30 a.m	Battn marched to chateau at CISSY and bathed in the lake.	NCA
"	8		Reconnaissance of BOVES area. Training under company arrangements.	NCA
"	9		Casualties 1 O.R. wounded by bomb dropped by enemy aeroplane.	NCA
"	9	11 a.m	Church Parade. Battn. ready to move on orders.	NCA
FLERS	10	12.30 p.m	Battn embussed at Briquemesnil and debussed at LE BOSQUEL. Marched to FLERS-SUR-NOYE arriving at 9.45 p.m.	Appendix C.
-SUR-NOYE	11		Reconnaissance by C.O. 6 mile route march by companies	NCA
"	12		Reconnaissance by C.O. Company training	NCA
"	13		Orders received to stand by ready for move	NCA

Army Form C. 2118.

WAR DIARY
or
INTELLIGENCE SUMMARY.
(Erase heading not required.)

Instructions regarding War Diaries and Intelligence Summaries are contained in F.S. Regs., Part II. and the Staff Manual respectively. Title pages will be prepared in manuscript.

Place	Date	Hour	Summary of Events and Information	Remarks and references to Appendices
FLERS-SUR-NOYE	13	10:30 p.m.	Battn. left Flers-sur-noye and marched to St Fuscien arriving 3 a.m. 14/6/18	NCA Appendix D.
St FUSCIEN	14	4 p.m.	Rifle inspection. Reconnaissance of support position.	NCA
"	15		Company training	NCA
"	16		Battn. marched by companies to CAGNY and bathed in river AVRE	NCA
"	17		} Company training	NCA
"	18			NCA
"	19			Appendix E. NCA
RUMAINSIL	20	5 p.m.	at 11 a.m. Battn. was relieved by 6th Battn. 224th French Regiment and marched to Rumainsil arriving 5 p.m.	Appendix F. NCA
AMPLIER	21	12 noon	At 4:10 a.m. marched to LOEUILLY Station arriving 6 a.m. Entrained at 8 a.m. Thence marched to Amplier arriving 1:30 p.m.	NCA
"	22	11:10 a.m.	Battn. ceremonial parade.	NCA
"	23	11:30 a.m.	Church parade	NCA Appendix G.
"	24		Company Training	NCA
SOUASTRE	25	11 p.m.	Entrained 11:30 a.m. arrived Souastre at 12 m.	NCA Appendix H.

WAR DIARY
or
INTELLIGENCE SUMMARY.
(Erase heading not required.)

Army Form C. 2118.

Place	Date	Hour	Summary of Events and Information	Remarks and references to Appendices
SOUASTRE	26		Baths and company training.	nca
"	27		Digging trench defences and company training.	nca
"	28			
"	29		Baths	nca
"	30		Church parade	nca

Appendix. A.

OPERATION ORDER NO. A

Copy No. 9

Ref: Sheet 57d 1/40000

(1). The enemy has penetrated our lines about ARRAS. The southern flank of his advance is bounded by the villages of TERRAMESNIL VAUCHELLES LES AUTHIE LOUVENCOURT BERTRANCOURT.
About VAUCHELLES LES AUTHIE his line runs O.2.b.6-8. O.3.b.5.8. O.4.b.2.8.

(2). On June 3rd.
A general counter attack will be made to gain the high ground South of the river AUTHIE. The 37th Division will attack with the 112th Inf: Brigade on the left and 111th Inf: Brigade on the right and capture the villages of VAUCHELLES LES AUTHIE and LOUVENCOURT and the high ground in @ I.27. and 28., while the 63rd Inf: Brigade passes through to capture the high ground South of the AUTHIE and the crossings in I.18.
The 112th Inf: Brigade will attack on a front of two battalions 1st ESSEX Regt; on right and 13th R.F. on left; The 1/1 HERTS. will be in support.
Boundaries and objectives are shown on map A.
Zero hour will be given at position of assembly.
The attack will pass through units holding our own front line, and be carried through according to the time table on Map A.

(3).
Position of assembly is in O.21.d. companies will be in close column of platoons in following order from the left:-
Y. W.
Z. X.
Distance and intervals between companies will be 100 paces.
"Y" Coy: will direct and will be at point of wood on track at O.21.d.1.3.
Battalion H.Q. will be at O.21.d.7.3.

(4).
The line of advance is grid north, and companies will move at Zero- 2 hours in artillery formation if possible to low ground in O.9.a. and b.
The section of machine guns allotted to the battalion will move forward with "W" Coy: to take up a position near BELLE EGLISE to cover the advance.
Battalion H.Q. will move behind "Z" Coy:

(5).
On deployment the leading companies will push through to the first objective timing advance so as to assault enemy front line at Zero.
One platoon each from "X" and "Z" companies will be detailed as moppers up to the assaulting waves and will consolidate enemy front line.
On gaining first objective strong patrols will be pushed out to railway line in I.33.b. and d.
Battalion H.Q. at Zero will be at O.3.d.5.8.

(6). At zero plus 40 minutes the leading Coys. will advance and capture the second objective and consolidate.

(7).
At zero plus one hour "X" & "Z" Coys. will pass through the second objective, move round the flank of the village and continue their advance to the final objective.
The village will be cleared by the 1/1 Herts. Battn.H.Q. will
Battn.H.Q. will be at I.33.c.9.1.

(8).
On reaching the final objective consolidation will commence and will consist of a series of section posts echeloned in depth.
Two strong points will be constructed at I.27.d.6.4. and I.27.d.1.8. for which assistance will be given by a section of the 153rd Field Coy.
Battn.H.Q. will be at I.27.d.40.

(9). Prisoners captured will be sent back to Battn.H.Q. walking wounded being used as escorts.
(10). Regimental Aid Post will be at Battn.H.Q.
(11). Watches will be synchronised at zero minus 2½ hours.

2/6/18.

CAPTAIN,
ADJUTANT 1st BN. THE ESSEX REGT.

DISTRIBUTION.

Copy No. 1 - B.H.Q.
" 2/5 - Coys.
" 6 - 112th Inf. Bde.
" 7 - Signal Officer.
" 8 - Transport Officer.
" 9 - War Diary.
" 10 - "

Issued at 8.45 p.m. by Orderly.

Appendix. C.

1st ESSEX OPERATION ORDER NO. 29.

Ref: Map   Copy No. 11
(ARRAS-1/100,000)   10/5/17.

1.   The Brigade will move by bus to the SOUTH Area this morning.

2.   Probable embussing time 10 a.m.

3.   Transport will move by road at 7 a.m.

4.   10% personnel will accompany unit.

5.   Dress: Full Marching Order, Steel Helmets on pack.

6.   Four Lewis Guns per Company, with proportion of ammunition, will be taken in the busses (which are French busses).

7.   Reconnaissance of 9th French Corps front by Major D.O'Gate Marsh, Lieut. W.D.Mathieson and 2/Lieut. H.Fairbank, is cancelled.

8.   Officers' Mess Kits, valises, etc. to be stacked at Q.M. Stores by 9.15 A.M.

9.   Billeting party of one other rank per Company (to be mounted on bicycles drawn from Q.M.Stores) including H.Q.Coy., will report to 2/Lieut.A.D.R.Davison at Battn.H.Q. at 7.15 a.m.

10.   All training arrangements are accordingly cancelled.

11.   Time of Battalion Parade will be notified later.

12.   No change in detail except Sick Parade on arrival at destination.

Later. Reveille 6 a.m. Breakfast 6.a.m. in view of Transport moving at 7 a.m.

Issued at 3.30 a.m.

P. Shah.
Captain & Adjutant
1st Battn.the Essex Regt.

Copy No. 1 - File
   " No. 2 - W. Coy.
   " No. 3 - X   "
   " No. 4 - Y   "
   " No. 5 - Z   "
   " No. 6 - H.Q.
   " No. 7 - M.O.
   " No. 8 - L.G.O.
   " No. 9 - I.O.
   " No.10 - R.S.M.
   " No.11 - War Diary
   " No.12 -   "

Appendix, D.

1ST ESSEX OPERATION ORDER NO. 30.

REF: MAP
AMIENS 17
1/100,000.

Copy No. 9
13/8/18.

1. The Battalion will march to ST. FUSCIEN (about 9 miles) via ORESMAUX - GRATTEPANCHE - SAINS.

2. Starting point - Church FLERS.

3. Order of March:
   H.Q., "Z" "X" "Y" "W" Transport.
   100 yards distance to be maintained between Coys.
   H.Q. will pass starting point at 10.30 p.m.

4. Lewis Gun Limbers will accompany Companies and signal equipment will be loaded on these limbers.

5. Kits and Mess Stores, etc. to be handed in at Q.M.Stores by 9.30 p.m.

6. Coys. will report arrival in new billets.

Issued at 7.30 p.m. by orderly.

H.Daly Lt.
Captain & Adjutant
1st Battn. the Essex Regt.

Copy No. 1 to 112th Inf.Bde.
"   "   2 " "W" Coy.
"   "   3 " "X" "
"   "   4 " "Y" "
"   "   5 " "Z" "
"   "   6 " T.O.
"   "   7 " Q.M.
"   "   8   War Diary.
"   "   9   "

War Diary   Appendix E

1ST ESSEX OPERATION ORDER NO. 51.

Map.Ref.   Copy No. 9
AMIENS 17   19/6/18.
1/100,000.

1. The Battalion will march to-morrow to RUMAISNIL (about 10½ miles) via SAINS - RUMIGNY - HEBECOURT - BOVES - Junction of road 1¼ miles north of u in PROUZEL.

2. Starting point - Battalion Alarm Post.

3. Order of march - "W" "H.Q" "Z" "X" "Y".

4. Lewis Gun limbers and other transport will move in rear of the battalion.
   2/Lieut.G.L.Kemp will be in charge of the transport.

5. Officers' Valises will be at Q.M.Stores by 8 a.m. Coy. Mess Boxes will travel on Coy. Cookers. Bands Packs, Office Stores, and H.Q.Mess Boxes will be ready to load on a lorry at 8 a.m. stacked by Chateau Gate.

6. Reveille - 6.45 a.m.
   Breakfast - 7.30 "
   Coys. will be ready to clear billets by 9 a.m.
   On the alarm sounding Coys. will fall in on the Battalion Alarm Post, transport on right of ST.FUSCIEN - SAINS Road facing south.

Issued at 9.45 p.m.

                                                    H.J.Young
                                                    Captain
                                        for Lieut.& adj.1st Battn.the Essex Regt.

Copy No. 1 - 115th Inf.Bde.
    "   2 - "W" Coy.
    "   3 - "X" "
    "   4 - "Y" "
    "   5 - "Z" "
    "   6 - T.O.
    "   7 - Q.M.
    "   8 - War Diary.
    "   9 - "

Appendix. F.

1ST ESSEX OPERATION ORDER NO. 22.

Map Ref:
AMIENS 57 1/100,000
& LENS 11 1/100,000.

Copy No. 9
20/6/18.

1.   The Battalion will move to-morrow by route march to LONGUILLY, entrain at 7.2 a.m., rail to MONDICOURT, and march thence to AUTHIEULE Area (E. of DOULLENS).
Order of march: "Y" "W" "H.Q." "Z" "X".

2.   Reveille   - 2.45 a.m.
      Breakfast   - 3.30 "
      Fall in   - 4.00 "
      March off   - 4.10 "
      Arrive Stn. - 5.30 "

3.   Transport, Chargers, Pack Animals & Cyclists will move at 7.0 a.m. to SALEUX and entrain thereat at 11.35 a.m. 2/Lieut. C.H.Kemp in charge of transport. Major Marsh, entraining officer for transport, will report to R.T.O., SALEUX, at 7.35 a.m.

4.   Captain H.J.Young will report to R.T.O., LONGUILLY, for entraining of personnel.

5.   Fires of Cookers will be drawn before entraining. 24 hours fuel will be carried; Water Carts will be full.

6.   A half lorry for surplus baggage will leave RUMAISNIL at 1 a.m.(approx.) for H.Q. Office furniture, H.Q.Officers' Mess Kit & Coy. Mess Boxes.
      This baggage must be stacked at Battn. Orderly Room ready to load by 11 p.m. to-night.

Issued at 8.45 p.m.

                                        Captain
                            for Lieut. & Adj. 1st Battn.the Essex Regt.

Copy No. 1 - 118th Inf. Bde.
 "   " 2 - "W" Coy.
 "   " 3 - "X" "
 "   " 4 - "Y" "
 "   " 5 - "Z" "
 "   " 6 - T.O.
 "   " 7 - Q.M.
 "   " 8 - War Diary.
 "   " 9 -   "

Appendix. G.

SECRET.

1ST ESSEX OPERATION ORDER No. 83.

Copy No. 11.

REF:MAP
SHEET 57D.1/40.000.

23/6/18.

1. (a)   The 37th Division is relieving the 62nd (W.R.) Division in the Left Sector of the IV Corps front between the 23rd and 26th June.

   (b)   Disposition of the 37th Division on completion of relief is to be:-
   Right Sector   — 111th Inf. Brigade.
   Left Sector   — 63rd Inf. Brigade.
   Divisional Reserve — 112th Inf. Brigade.

2. (a)   The 112th Infantry Brigade will relieve the 185th Infantry Brigade as Brigade in Divisional Reserve on the morning of June 25th.

   (b)   The 1st Essex Regiment will hand over to the 1/5th Devon Regiment and will take over from the 9th West Yorks Regiment at SOUASTRE (VALLEY CAMP).

3.   The Battalion will move by bus. be
         Hour of embussing will probably ^ 10 a.m.

4. (a)   A reconnoitring party composed of 2/Lieut.N.C.Ahrens, 2/Lieut.A.L.Bryant "X" Coy. and two other ranks, one to be detailed by the Quartermaster and one by the Transport Officer, will proceed at 9 a.m. on the 24th instant. Names of two other ranks to be in Orderly Room by 9 p.m. 23/6/18. These two men will remain at SOUASTRE.

   (b)   Transport arrangements for this party will be notified later.

Issued at 7.30 p.m.by runner.

H. Daly
Lieutenant
A/Adjutant 1st Batn.the Essex Regt.

```
Copy No.  1 - 112th Inf. Bde.
  "    "   2 - "W" Coy.
  "    "   3 - "X"  "
  "    "   4 - "Y"  "
  "    "   5 - "Z"  "
  "    "   6 - Q.M.
  "    "   7 - I.O.
  "    "   8 - T.O.
  "    "   9 - R.S.M.
  "    "  10 - War Diary.
  "    "  11 -    "
```

SECRET.
Appendix. H.

ADDENDUM TO OPERATION ORDER No. 35.

Date: 24/8/18.   Copy No. 12

1. (a)   The Battalion will move by Bus to-morrow.

   (b)   Twenty-nine busses (Nos.1/29) each carrying 25 men are at the disposal of the Battalion.

   (c)   Embussing Point - DOULLENS - BARLY Road.
         Head at Cross roads N.3.a.2.2. facing East.
         Embussing time 11.30 a.m.

2. (a)   Companies will move to Embussing Point in following order - "Z" "Y" "X" "W" B.H.Q. and will be drawn up on the southern side of road by 11.30 a.m., told off in bus parties, with head of B.H.Q. at Cross Roads N.3.a.2.2.

   (b)   "Z" Company will pass starting point at N.3.a.2.2. at 11.30 a.m.

   (c)   Each bus takes up 10 yards of road when halted. A gap of 20 yards is left between each 9 busses.

3.   Captain H.J.Young will act as Embussing Officer, and will report to Lieut.A.H.Austin,M.C. at Cross Roads N.3.a.2.2. ½ hour before the embussing hour.

4.   Officers will be distributed along the column, as far as possible one to each bus.

5.   Debussing Point will be Road Triangle D.21.b.2.0.- D.21.b.9.8.- D.22.a.6.9.

6.   Surplus personnel being left out of the line will remain in present billets to-morrow. Further instructions on this point will follow.

Issued at 7.30 p.m.

                                                    K.Daly
                                                    Lieutenant
                                                    A/Adjutant 1st Battn.the Essex Regt.

         Distribution.

         To all recipients of Operation Order No.35.

CONFIDENTIAL.

WAR DIARY

OF

1ST BATTALION THE ESSEX REGIMENT

FOR

JULY, 1918.

VOLUME 41.

Army Form C. 2118.

WAR DIARY
INTELLIGENCE SUMMARY.
(Erase heading not required.)

Instructions regarding War Diaries and Intelligence Summaries are contained in F. S. Regs., Part II. and the Staff Manual respectively. Title pages will be prepared in manuscript.

Place	Date	Hour	Summary of Events and Information	Remarks and references to Appendices
SOUASTRE	July 1		Training under company arrangements and digging parties working on CHATEAU — DE-LA HAIE Switch.	
"	2	8 a.m	Range Practice during the morning. Batts marched from SOUASTRE at 8 p.m and relieved 16th Battn Royal Fusiliers in front line BUCQUOY. Relief completed at 1 a.m 3/7/18.	Officers
"	"			
BUCQUOY	3		W. and Y. Company front line X and Z supports furnished working parties. 2 ORs Wounded.	
"	4		Usual working Parties	
"	5		"	
"	6	10.30 p.m.	Inter Company Relief. - 1.O.R. Wounded	
"	7		Working Parties 4 ORs Wounded, + 1.O.R. Killed	
"	8		Working Parties 2. O.R. Wounded.	
"	9		Enemy attempt to Raid on our posts west corn of T.M. Emplacement Raid unsuccessful.	
"	10		4. O.R. Wounded. Working Parties.	

Army Form C. 2118.

WAR DIARY
or
INTELLIGENCE SUMMARY
(Erase heading not required.)

Instructions regarding War Diaries and Intelligence Summaries are contained in F. S. Regs., Part II. and the Staff Manual respectively. Title pages will be prepared in manuscript.

Place	Date	Hour	Summary of Events and Information	Remarks and references to Appendices
Bucquoy	July 10	9.30 p.m.	The Battalion was relieved by the 13th R.F. went back into Support at Pigeon Wood. Relief complete 2.0. a.m. 11.7.18.	Appendix 2 attached.
Pigeon Wood	11		Working Parties. 2 O.R. Wounded.	
	12		3 O.R. Wounded. Digging Strong Point in Biez Wood. 4 O.R. Wounded.	
	13		Working Parties. Battalion was relieved by the 8th S.L.I. The Battalion proceeded to Valley Camp, Souastre. Relief complete 2.0 a.m. riffle attacked	Appendix 3 attached
	"		Scheme for Raid on Right Subsector South of Bucquoy drawn up by :- Lt. Col. A.R.C. Sanders C.M.G. D.S.O. C.C. 7th Essex Regt. The Scheme was accepted by Division + carried out by the 4th Middlesex Regt. night of the 23/7/18. with success	Appendix attached.
Souastre	14		Battalion Baths	
	15		Parties under Company arrangements.	
	16.	8.30 p.m.	The Battalion relieved the 1/1st Herts Regt. in Reserve to the Right Brigade Fonquevillers (Le "Z") Relief complete m.n. attached.	Appendix 5
Le "Z"	17		Working Parties	
	18		" + 1 O.R. Killed + 1 O.R. Wounded	

WAR DIARY
or
INTELLIGENCE SUMMARY.
(Erase heading not required.)

Army Form C. 2118.

Instructions regarding War Diaries and Intelligence Summaries are contained in F. S. Regs., Part II. and the Staff Manual respectively. Title pages will be prepared in manuscript.

Place	Date	Hour	Summary of Events and Information	Remarks and references to Appendices
The "Z" Essarts.	July. 19		Working Parties making Dug. outs.	appendix
	20		Battalion relieved the 13th R.B.s in appendix to Support to the Left Sector Div' front. Relief complete 11.30 pm attached	
	21		Working Parties	
	22		"	
	23		"	
	24		Battalion relieved 13th R.F.s in Left Subsector. Brigade front appendix Relief complete 1.0 am. (25/7/16) X + Z Front line attached W + Y Support. 1. o.r. Killed.	
Aloinzeville	25		Holding Line.	
	26		" 2.or. Wounded.	
	27		" 2.or. Wounded.	
	28	11.30 pm	Inter Company relief	
	29		Working Parties 4.OR. Wounded.	
	30		Working Parties. 1.O.R. Wounded.	

WAR DIARY
or
INTELLIGENCE SUMMARY.
(Erase heading not required.)

Army Form C. 2118.

Place	Date	Hour	Summary of Events and Information	Remarks and references to Appendices
Ablainzevelle	July 31	1.15am	Scheme for Raid attacked. The Raid was not as successful as might have been owing to a Barrage falling on the forward wave after the first objective. Our casualties were 2/Lt B. Plant Wounded. 3 O.R. Killed & 18 O.R. Wounded. 2 missing	Appendix 8. Attached.

Appendix I

SECRET.
1ST ESSEX OPERATION ORDER No. 54.

Copy No.

REF: MAP
57.D.N.E.
1/20,000

1/7/18.

(1)   The 118th Infantry Brigade will relieve the 111th Infantry Brigade in Right Sector of the Divisional Front on the night 2/3rd July, 1918.

(2)   1st Essex Regt. will relieve the 10th Royal Fusiliers in the Left Subsector BUCQUOY, as under :-
Front line from right to left:
"W" Coy.   "Y" Coy.
  Support   "X" "
  Reserve   "Z" "

(3)   Guides for front line Coys. will be at junction of railway and road at F.26.c.2.6.
      Guides for H.Q., Support & Reserve Coys., will be at cross roads south of ESSARTS F.19.c.8.2.

(4)   Order of March :
      H.Q. "W" "X" "Y" "Z"
      Platoons at 200 yards interval.
      Route: WILLOW PATCH, MAILLYCAMPS, ESSARTS Road.

(5)   H.Q. Coy. will pass starting point, road junction eastern exit of SOUASTRE D.22.b.9.5. at 8·0 pm.

(6)   Completion of relief will be reported by code words of the Coy. Commanders names.

(7)   Surplus kits & stores will be dumped at Q.M.Stores by 6 p.m.

(8)   Water from the well at BUCQUOY is not fit for drinking.

(9)   Receipts for Trench Stores, in duplicate, will be forwarded to B.H.Q. by 6 a.m. 3rd instant.

                              [signature]
                              Lieut. Col.
                  Commdg. 1st Battn.the Essex Regt.

Copy No. 1 - 118th Inf.Bde.
   "   2 - "W" Coy.
   "   3 - "X" "
   "   4 - "Y" "
   "   5 - "Z" "
   "   6 - 10th R.F.
   "   7 - Q.M.
   "   8 - M.O.
   "   9 - War Diary.
   "   10 - "
   "   11 - R.S.M.

SCHEME FOR RAID

IN RIGHT SUBSECTOR SOUTH OF BUCQUOY IN L.2.d.

1. The object of the raid is to secure an identification.

2. **Ground.** The ground S.W. of the village slopes more steeply from the 150 contour into the valley running East from the corner of BIEZ WOOD, consequently the enemy's trenches about L.2.d.8.3. are defiladed from the enemy's posts about the Western outskirts of the village. Similarly the ground in front of the posts F.G.H. from a gentle slope falls more steeply into the valley South of BUCQUOY. The enemy has taken advantage of this convex slope and has sited his posts and wire in rear, and they are consequently invisible from our outpost line.

    The Spur running from ROSSIGNOL WOOD to PUISIEUX affords observation over the locality of the proposed raid and would therefore have to be masked.

    A smoke screen down the valley running East from the corner of BIEZ WOOD is facilitated by the accidents of the ground.

3. **Enemy dispositions.** By night the enemy is alert and pushes forward listening posts about the BUCQUOY-HEBUTERNE road to cover his machine guns.

    These posts appear to be withdrawn by day, but the trench in rear appears to be held by day, more especially the post at the end of the road about L.2.d.15.05, and at the point of the triangle about L.2.d.70.35.

    Troops in support appear to be in the sunken road BUCQUOY PUISIEUX 3 to 400 yards in rear.

4. **Forming up.** The present outpost line affords ample facilities for forming up the raiding party and can be reached by day.

    Several dugout shafts exist where men could be accommodated and where it would probably be better for the raiding party to remain on completion of raid if enemy barrage was heavy or fire was directed on the O.T's.

5. **S.O.S.Line.** The enemy S.O.S. line appears to be on the HEBUTERNE BUCQUOY road which corresponds with our outpost line. Enemy T.M's. would open early, but hostile artillery is generally late in starting and chiefly consists of field guns.

6. **Wire.** The enemy is busy wiring and owing to the ground being defiladed it is difficult to observe wire cutting.

    Patrol reports do not show much wire in the vicinity of the road, but the ground is cut up by shell holes.

7. **Raiding Party.** It is suggested the party should consist of 48 men. 2 parties of 10 to hold the terminal points at L.3.c.05.30 and L.2.d.15.05, while 4 parties of 7 each mop up the intervening trench.

8. **Success.** Success can only lie in surprise and consequently rapidity of action is essential. Although the attack is down hill into the valley, it is considered that the advantages of daylight in crossing broken and largely unknown ground, provided the right flank is obscured by smoke, and our barrage is directed on the right targets, will ensure the necessary rapidity of movement.

    Darkness while screening movement militates against cohesion of attack and disorganises it if an unknown obstacle is encountered.

    If little wire has been erected and raiding parties can move out on taped lines, a night surprise is possible, but the enemy dispositions in forward listening posts guard against this.

    By day these posts are withdrawn. The quietest time appears to be 1.20 p.m. - English time as batteries come into action about 2 p.m.

(2)

9. **Targets.**   The accompanying map shows the necessary artillery targets.

Special care is required in engaging Trech Mortars from North of BUCQUOY to FORK WOOD. Enemy Machine Guns in the sunken road (held by the supports) on the high ground East of the village of BUCQUOY and North of PUISIEUX must also be engaged.

Machine Gun fire would materially assist, in conjunction with the smoke screen down the valley on the right flank of the raid.

10.   The scheme is based on a personal reconnaissance and an interview with the unit holding the line, this regiment not having held the sector.

13/7/18.

                                                    Lieut. Col.
Commdg. 1st Battn. the Essex Regiment.

Appendix 5

1ST ESSEX OPERATION ORDER NO. 57.

REF. MAP
SHEET 57 D.
1/40,000.

Copy No. 10

16/7/18.

(1) The Battalion will relieve the 1/1st Herts. Regt., which is in reserve to the right Brigade, on the night of the 16/17th July.

(2) The Battalion will move by platoons at 200 yards interval. Starting point: Entrance to VALLEY CAMP on the HENU – SOUASTRE Road. Route: SOUASTRE – FONQUEVILLERS Road.

(3) Order of March: H.Q. "Z" "Y" "X" "W" relieving respectively H.Q. Nos. 4, 1, 3, and 2 Coys.
H.Q. will pass starting point at 8.45 p.m.

(4) One limber for H.Q. and each Coy. will report at respective H.Q. at 8.15 p.m.

(5) Guides from 1/1st Herts. Regt. will be at FONQUEVILLERS Church at 9.30 p.m.

(6) Completion of relief will be reported by code words "Nothing doing".

Issued at 5.15 p.m.

H Daly
Lieutenant
A/Adjutant 1st Battn. the Essex Regt.

Copy No. 1 – 118th Inf. Bde.
" " 2 – "W" Coy.
" " 3 – "X" "
" " 4 – "Y" "
" " 5 – "Z" "
" " 6 – T.O.
" " 7 – O.C.
" " 8 – R.M.O.
" " 9 – War Diary.
" " 10 – "

SCHEME FOR RAID NORTH OF BUCQUOY IN F.28.b. & d.
==

(1) **Object** of raid is to obtain identifications.

(2) **Ground.** From the shape of the ground it appears that the objective is defiladed from the CEMETERY and the CRUCIFIX, but well under view from ABLAINZEVELLE. The enemy's outpost line appears to be sited just behind the crest of the spur, and consequently observation is difficult to obtain.

(3) **Enemy Organisation.** The outpost line appears lightly held with listening posts pushed out in front of his Machine Guns. The line of resistance is on average 150 yards in rear and a supporting point is situated 200 yards in rear again. This appears to be an old battery position.
   ABLAINZEVELLE and the reentrant immediately to the South appear to be strongly held, but no reserves are in the immediate vicinity and probably not nearer than LOGEAST WOOD.

(4) **Wire.** is reported as continuous and consisting of a double concertina belt mixed with knife rests.

(5) **Boundaries.** The objective is clearly defined by the line of the railway on the South and by the track running from F.30.b.05 to the road and trench junction at F.29.a.85.40. This will facilitate barrage lines and objectives for our Machine Guns and Lewis Guns.

(6) **Objectives.**
   Outpost line from railway line F.29.d.77 to F.29.a.00.85 "A")
   Main line from railway line F.29.c.0.7 to F.29.a.5.2.   "B")
   Sumpit at F.29.a.5.2.   Centre   "C")
   A frontage of 500 yards and centre covered by artillery now in)
   position.

(7) **Raiding Party.**   2 sections for outpost line on flanks.
                         2 sections for main line on flanks.
                         1 section central in support with O.C. raiders.
                         2 sections on Sumpit (possibly one section).
   Total: 1 Officer 7 N.C.O's. 48 O.R's.

(8) **Cutting Wire.** To cut wire it is proposed that from Zero - 5 night to Zero - 1 night.parties will lay Bungalore torpedoes along whole front. Artillery fire will be subsequently opened on these points with the view to keeping them open and induce the enemy to believe that wire cutting is undertaken so as to cause loss to repairing parties.
   Owing to these operations and the moon being favourable, it is expected that increased vigilance by night will be ordered and this will lead to a corresponding increase in sleepiness by day.

(9) Time of raid is proposed at 3 p.m. on Zero day.

(10) **Barrage times and lifts:**
   From Zero to Zero   3 minutes on A.B.C.
   At Zero + 3 minutes lift from A. to B.
   At Zero + 3 minutes lift from B. to Box barrage.
   To Zero + 4 minutes lift from C. to Box barrage.

(11) **Other Targets for Artillery.**
   Re-entrant trenches in F.29.a. particularly at F.29.a.80.70 and 75.45.
   Quarry to Coy. H.Q. in ABLAINZEVELLE.
   Gas and Smoke to be used in conjunction.

(2)

Trench Mortars.
(F.23.c.85.83. F.23.d.95.95. F.23.d.05.95. F.23.d.15.90.
(F.23.d.25.42. F.23.c.75.60. F.23.c.80.40. F.23.b.00.20.

F.29.a.90.70. F.29.d.60.05.

L.4.a.38.00. L.3.d.70.95. L.3.d.70.70. L.3.d.15.88.
L.3.b.90.70. L.3.d.70.50.

Machine Guns - L.4.b.85.35.

Batteries. Batteries are usually slow in opening fire principal ones to be neutralised if fire is opened appear to be in A.7 zone probably a selection from A.7 1, 15, 7, 8, 17, 6, 5 and 20.

Machine Guns. To fire on trenches and posts south of the railway down to the cemetery and Crucifix and on reentrant trenches south of ABLAINZEVELLE.

Signal of return

Raiding Party will practice at SOUASTRE. Administrative instructions will follow if raid is approved.

19/7/18.

[signature]
Lieut. Col.
Commdg. 1st Battn. the Essex Regt.

1st Essex Operation Order No 38. (6)

Ref: Sheet   Copy No. 6
57D N.E. 1/20,000.

1. The 112th Inf: Bde. will relieve the 111th Inf Bde in the Left Section of the Divisional front on the night of 20/21st July.

2. The 1st Essex Regt will relieve the 13th Rifle Brigade in Support Batt'n Area.

3. The relief will take place in the following order:- H.Qrs. X. Z. W. Y. Companies will take over as follows:-
"W" Coy will relieve "A"   "X" Coy will relieve "B"
"Y" "   "   "D"   "Z" "   "   "C"
H.Qrs will move at 9.25 pm.
200 yards distance between platoons will be maintained.
Guides will meet Coys as follows:-
    W & Y Coys where road crosses railway in ESSARTS (near present "Z" Coy HQ)
    "X" Coy. where trench crosses road 200 yards West of ESSARTS Crucifix.
    "Z" Coy at HALIFAX POST.

4. One officer per Coy & B'n HQ. and one N.C.O per platoon and B'n HQ. will move in advance to the Batt'n. to be relieved.

4 cont:

These parties will report direct to Bn. HQ. 13th R.B. at E.24.d.80.80. at 9am 19th inst.

5. All trench stores, defence schemes, maps etc will be taken over & those for present area handed over to representative of incoming unit.

6. Completion of relief will be notified by code word "All quiet".

Issued by Orderly
4 pm 18.7.18.

H. Daly Lieut.
a/Adj 1/Essex Regt.

Copy no 1. to 112th Inf Bde
" " 2 " W Coy
" " 3 " X "
" " 4 " Y "
" " 5 " Z "
" " 6 " I.O.
" " 7 " T.O.
" " 8 " } War Diary
" " 9 "

Operation Order No 3/ (7)

1. Ref Sheet   Copy No. 7
   57D N.E. 1/20.000.

1) The Battalion will relieve the 13th R.F. in the Left Subsector of the Brigade Front on the night of 24/25th July.

2) Companies will take over sectors as already detailed.

3) The relief will take place in the following order:—
   13th H.Q. will move at 9.30 pm.
   "Z" Coy   "   "   9.40 pm.
   "X" "   "   "   9.50 pm.
   "W" & "Y"   "   "   9.40 pm.

   200 yards distance will be maintained between Platoons.

4. Guides (2 for B.H.Q. + 5 per Coy.) will meet as follows:—
   "Z" Coy at Junction of BADEN and TOP TRENCH F.22.a.1.5.
   "X" Coy at Junction of TOP TRENCH and PRUSSIAN AVENUE F.21.c.60.25.
   B.H.Q. "W" & "Y" Coys at Junction of ROAD and ARTILLERY TRENCH F.20.a.30.15
   Post guides will be arranged by Company Commanders.

   P.T.O.

5. Petrol cans from B.H.Q. and all Coys will be dumped on sunken road where ARTILLERY TRENCH crosses it. F.20.a.30.15.
   One man from each Coy will be left as a guard & to get receipts.
6. Ration limbers tonight will be on road near new B.H.Q. at 11.30 P.M.
   Support Coys will carry rations to forward Coy H.Q. but forward Coys will send guide to B.H.Q. to guide them down.
7. Mutual receipts for taking over & handing over will be given & received
8. Completion of relief will be notified by Code word "NIL RETURN".

Issued at 3.30 pm
by Orderly

                            Lieut
                          7/Adj 1/Essex Regt.

Copy No 1 to 112 Inf Bde
"   2 " O.C. W
"   3 " "   X
"   4 " "   Y
"   5 " "   Z
"   6 " T.O & Q.M
"   7 " War Diary.

CONFIDENTIAL 112/37

WAR DIARY

OF

1ST BATTN THE ESSEX REGT

FOR

AUGUST, 1918

VOLUME 42.

WAR DIARY

Army Form C. 2118.

Place	Date	Hour	Summary of Events and Information	Remarks and references to Appendices
Top Trench AUHINVILLERS	Aug. 1	2 p.m.	Batt was Relieved by the 8th Lincolns. Relief Complete 10 am 2/9/13. Returned to Souastre.	Appendix 1 attached
"	"	10.0	to Valley Comp. Souastre. 1 O.R. Killed	
"	2		Batt Baths	NCR
"	3		Working Parties, Baths & Parades under Company arrangements.	NCR
"	4		Church Parade	NCR Appendix 2 attached
the "Z"	5	10.0 p.m.	Relieved the 13th R.F. in the 'Z' Essarts Sector. Relief complete 11.0 p.m.	NCR
"	6		Working Parties	NCR
"	7		" "	NCR
"	8		" "	NCR
"	9		" Baths at Fonquevillers	
Bucquoy	9		" Batt moved up to Bucquoy Sector 9.30 p.m. Relieved the 13th K.R.R.C. Relief complete 1.0 am 10/9/18. 1. O.R. Wounded	Appendix 3 attached
"	10		Working parties 3. O.Rs. Wounded	NCR
"	11		" " 1. O.R. "	NCR
"	12		" "	NCR
"	13	6.6 am	Gas Projector attack launched with success on our front 2 O.Rs Wounded	

WAR DIARY
or
INTELLIGENCE SUMMARY.
(Erase heading not required.)

Army Form C. 2118.

Instructions regarding War Diaries and Intelligence Summaries are contained in F.S. Regs., Part II. and the Staff Manual respectively. Title pages will be prepared in manuscript.

Place	Date	Hour	Summary of Events and Information	Remarks and references to Appendices
Bucquoy	Aug 14	P.m. 1.30	3 Prisoners Captured of the 91st Bavarian Regt. by "W" Company	
			2. ORs Killed 5. ORs Wounded. Inter Company Relief.	WA
	15		Working Parties	WA
	16		Advanced our Outpost Line. 6. ORs Wounded 1 Killed	
	"		Position held. Our Captures included 2 Light Machine Guns, 1 Very Light Pistol, Rifles & Documents.	WA
	17		The Enemy Raided our "K" Post & was Repulsed	WA
	18		Reorganised New Brigade Boundary	WA
	19		Relieved by 8th S.L.I. Relief Complete 1.30 am 20/8/18	WA Appendix 4 attached
Nouveillers	20		Battⁿ moved back to Foogúvillers arriving 3.0 am	WA
	"	P.m 9.30	Baths	
Durham Trench	"		Battⁿ moved up to Durham Trench	
Halifax Trench	21		Operations of 63rd & 111th Bde Successful. Battⁿ Withdrew to Halifax Trench to await Orders.	WA
	22	"	After a Conference at Bde HQ at 6.0 Am instructions were received for an early advance & an attack through the 63rd Divⁿ	

Army Form C. 2118.

WAR DIARY
or
~~INTELLIGENCE SUMMARY.~~
(Erase heading not required.)

Instructions regarding War Diaries and Intelligence Summaries are contained in F. S. Regs., Part II. and the Staff Manual respectively. Title pages will be prepared in manuscript.

Place	Date	Hour	Summary of Events and Information	Remarks and references to Appendices
	22		At 7.0 p.m. a conference of Coy commanders was called & the probable situation with objectives explained	
	"	P.m. 10-30	The Battn. moved off by Platoons via Bucquoy the track parallel to the Light Railway from Bucquoy to LOGEAST WOOD thence Achiet-le-Petit Reach to trenches in G.8. Two Coys were in the front line & 2 were in support.	
	23		The Battn. were in position about 3.30 am the front being still held by the Artists Rifles, 63rd Division.	appendix 5 attached
	"		An Officers Patrol failed the gain touch with the 37th Division on Achiet-le-petit on its troops had been withdrawn from the Village	
	"		About 9.0 am orders were received for the attack to start at 11.0 am.	
	"		This gave very little time for the issue of orders or reconnaissance.	
	"		A warning order was sent out at once followed by operation orders which reached Coys about 10.30 am. The attack was made in four waves the two Coys in front line & Support each forming two waves in following order from the right Y W Z X.	

Army Form C. 2118.

WAR DIARY
or
INTELLIGENCE SUMMARY
(Erase heading not required.)

Instructions regarding War Diaries and Intelligence Summaries are contained in F. S. Regs., Part II. and the Staff Manual respectively. Title pages will be prepared in manuscript.

Place	Date	Hour	Summary of Events and Information	Remarks and references to Appendices
	23	A.M. 11.0	Our Barrage opened + Coys moved forward to take up positions as close to the Barrage line (Road G.14.b. — G.15.a) as possible	
	"	A.M. 11.4	The Enemy Barrage opened roughly on a line from G.14.b.1.5 to G.9.c.0.5 + on the trenches vacated by the attacking Coys.	
	"	A.M. 11.8	Our Barrage lifted + the advance was steady + uninterrupted until the right flank reached a point about 250 yds over the road (G.14.b.5.5.) where it came under heavy machine gun + rifle fire from the ridge in front. The left flank was able to push on to the Summit of the Crest in G.15.a + b before coming under direct M.G. fire + some men even penetrated through Gaps in the wire to the Trench at G.15. Central. No further advance was possible + the right flank was in the air owing to the delay in advance by the 3rd Division on our Right + Severe losses were incurred from M.G. fire from the Trench in G.15.Central the ridge behind the Railway + from a derelict Tank at G.14.b.6.5. (approx) Supporting Coys had pushed forward into the firing	

WAR DIARY or INTELLIGENCE SUMMARY

Army Form C. 2118.

Place	Date	Hour	Summary of Events and Information	Remarks and references to Appendices
	23		line + units were mixed up. A party of about 20 men under 2/Lt E.P.Bugg attempted to rush forward but failed 2/Lt E.P.Bugg + majority of Party being killed or wounded. Messages were sent back by Capt Mathieson for the assistance of a Tank + about 1.37 P.m. One Tank came up from the Left Flank + started firing into the houses at G. is Central. There was an immediate decrease in the hostile fire + Capt. Mathieson immediately took advantage of the situation + carried the Trench. 2/Lt Sefton organised the Left Flank + Capt Mathieson + 2/Lt Buxton the right flank whilst a party under 2/Lt Mrs had also gained the Trench. Action was also made to the Railway line. Little resistance being made with the Railway gained about 7.0 P.m. A Patrol under 2/Lt Sefton was sent up the line of Trenches parallel to gain touch with the Troops on our	

Place	Date	Hour	Summary of Events and Information	Remarks and references to Appendices
	23		left but failed to do so, wd/, Cpt Mathieson pushed on with a strong Patrol up to the Sunken Rd in G.21.b, & on to the X Rds at G.22.a.5.2. There were no signs of the enemy except 4 Guns which had been hastily abandoned at G.22.a.5.1. Touch had been gained with the 182 Bde & 5th Division at G.21.a.9.2. 3 Coys moved forward to the trench in G.21.b. & 16.c. 1 Coy being left at the Rd + Rly crossing. A party of about 12 men from the 1/11th Kents also bivouac'd up at the X Rds G.22.a.5.1. Posts were then established by Cpt Mathieson as under:— Two covering the X Rds One covering the Right flank One covering the left flank and 3 in rear, one at the Camouflage Dug out on Rd, one at the Tank G.22.a.1.7. + 1 about G.21.b.9.5. Gun pits being completed the Party of 1/11th Kents en bivouac.	

WAR DIARY
or
INTELLIGENCE SUMMARY

(Erase heading not required.)

Army Form C. 2118.

Place	Date	Hour	Summary of Events and Information	Remarks and references to Appendices
	23	p.m. 5.25	Orders were received to continue the advance under a barrage starting at 5.30 P.m. Parties were pushed forward at 5.45 P.m. & lined up under the ridge in G.22.a. & c. On pressing over the ridge troops were seen retiring on our left & as the 5th Div had not moved heavy M.G. fire was experienced from the Right. The line was consequently withdrawn to that previously occupied.	
	24	p.m. 7.30	The 5th Div moved forward & came up into line with the posts in G.22.a. Touch was gained with them during the enemy & the position was consolidated. While on the Ridge the enemy was observed withdrawing his guns & fire was opened on them. Casualties being covered. Search was made for dead & wounded & Salvage was collected. From the enemy orders were received to push forward & occupy the line in F.23. A personal reconnaissance showed that the area mentioned as the	

WAR DIARY
or
INTELLIGENCE SUMMARY

Army Form C. 2118.

Place	Date	Hour	Summary of Events and Information	Remarks and references to Appendices
	24		ground was occupied by N.Z. Troops. The 2 role was consequently countermanded.	
	25		Salvage continued & a large amount of material was returned.	
	"	p.m. 10.0	Orders were received to move forward in Support of the 111th Bde & the Battalion passed the Starting Point at 11.30 p.m. B.H.Q. + 3 Coys went in the neighbourhood of the Monument near Bapaume + 1 Coy was near the Shrine	Appendix 6. W.M.
	26	a.m. 6.0	Information was received from G.O.C. 111th Bde. the Bde had been relieved.	
	"	p.m. 2.0	The Battn moved back to Achiet-le-Grand + came under the orders of the 112th Inf Bde.	
			Our Battle Casualties from the 21st to 26/8/18 inclusive were:—	
			3 Officers killed 2/Lt H.J. Witcombe 2/Lt J.E. Broad 2/Lt S.J. Wright	
			1 Officer died of wounds 2/Lt L.P. Reeves	

WAR DIARY
INTELLIGENCE SUMMARY
(Erase heading not required.)

Army Form C. 2118.

Instructions regarding War Diaries and Intelligence Summaries are contained in F.S. Regs., Part II. and the Staff Manual respectively. Title pages will be prepared in manuscript.

Place	Date	Hour	Summary of Events and Information	Remarks and references to Appendices
	26		Battle Casualties continued	
		10	Officers Wounded Capt L.J. Miles M.C.	
			Capt W.H. Macaulay	
			Lt C. H. Campling	MC
			2/Lt H. Fairbank	
			" A.J. Pearson	
			" A.L. Bryant	
			" E.P. Bugg.	
			" L.H.M. Wilcox	
			" J.E. Barrett	MC
			" S.D. McLoughlin	
			Other Ranks 78 killed 197 Wounded (although wounded) 8 Missing	
			remained with the unit.	
Lt. Grant 27th	27		Baths & Clean change. Resting in Reserve. Received Reinforcements	
	28		Burying Dead Received Draft of 243 Reinforcements	MC
	29		Salvaging	
	30		Training under Company Arrangements	
	31		Training Draft of 1 Officer.	

Copy: SECRET

5th Division
Operations on the 23rd August

Attack by the 15th and 95th Infantry Brigades (morning of 23rd)

The attack took place at 11 a.m.

On account of the short time available the barrage had been arranged on an arbitrary line, and owing to the exact map locations of the trenches not being known, the barrage was a little too far ahead of the infantry at the start, and was consequently lost in places. The front of attack on the left was a glacis-like slope as far as the railway, and a similar slope up the other side. The valley on the right of the attack across the railway was cut up by banks and tranches. In addition there was a trench running the whole length of the far crest about half way up and the valley towards the level crossing was full of machine guns which swept the whole front of the attack. Three lines of wire on the left constituted a serious obstacle before the railway was reached. Gaps had to be looked for, and it was here that many casualties to Officers occurred. In fact the left of the attack was completely held up for a time, and it was not until two tanks working in front of the 37th Division had nearly gained the crest, and put out many enemy M.Gs. that the advance could resumed. These Tanks, and the magnificent advance of the 37th Division, who had only relieved the 63rd Division during the previous night, on our left, undoubtedly allowed the 1st Bedfords to gain their final objective. Lt. Col. Courtenay, Commanding the battalion, himself personally pushed in two platoons at the critical moment and took the ridge. This gallant Officer was unfortunately killed, as were 9 other Officers of the battalion. Two companies of the 1st Norfolks were put in to thicken the line on the left, which was then successfully consolidated. About the same time 1st E. Surreys (Lt. Col. Minogus) gained their final objective on the right, but the 12th Gloucesters were held up just short of IRLES, being shot in the back from L.36.

It is impossible to realise the difficulty of the whole of the attack on the 23rd without seeing the ground. The determination with which the railway embankment on the right was tackled can be judged from the fact that over 25 machine guns were captured on a 50 yards front, and in another portion of the railway one platoon of the 1st E. Surreys worked round a small trench and captured 100 prisoners and twelve machine guns. Over 150 M.Gs. in all were captured by the right Brigade. One of the ravines opposite this Brigade was known by the Germans as the "AUGSBURG M.G. Strong point" (MASCHINEN GEWEHR STUTZPUNKT).

The whole attack was a very gallant piece of work; the advance of the 16th R. Warwickshire Regt. without a check to their final objective, with a formiable trench system running both at right angles to, and across, their line, was especially brilliant. The battalion was commanded by Lt. Col. Deakin, who on the day of the original attack had taken a few men across the railway and from the top of a mound by the level crossing had himself shot down the gunners serving a 5.9" battery which was firing point blank at the advancing troops of the 95th Infantry Brigade.

The enemy fought skillfully and made good use of their machine guns until we came to grips with them, when they surrendered freely.

37th Division No.G.215/141

1st Septr 1918

The above extract from 5th Division Report on Operations is forwarded for your information.

Sgd Wm. Anderson Major G.S.
for Lieut Colonel
General Staff 37th Division.

Army Form C. 2118.

WAR DIARY
or
INTELLIGENCE SUMMARY
(Erase heading not required.)

1. Essex Rgt. 11/2/37
Vol 34

34 N.

Place	Date	Hour	Summary of Events and Information	Remarks and references to Appendices
ACHIET-LE-GRAND	1st Sept /18		Training of Lewis Gunners under Company arrangements.	7.M.
"	2nd		Battalion Field Day. Based on the attack	nil
LEBUCQUIÈRE	3rd	2 pm	The Battalion moved up from ACHIET-LE-GRAND + relieved the 1st Bat'n CHESHIRE Reg't in LEBUCQUIÈRE, Hqrs at Jig d.4.0. CASUALTY - 1. O.R. wounded.	7.M. 7.0M.
E. of VELU	4th		The following morning the Bat'n was in position at 7.a.m. in J.26 central in support to the 15th ROYAL FUSILIERS + 1/1 HERTS, attacking HAVRINCOURT WOOD the attack being held up + touch with the N.Z. DIVISION on the right being lost, "Y" Coy was ordered forward to protect the RIGHT FLANK of the 1/1 HERTS and took up position in SUNKEN ROAD Pt central thus filling the gap. The remainder of the Bat'n occupied TRENCHES in J.33 and 34. Two prisoners were captured by "Y" Coy. CASUALTIES - 1 O.R. wounded + 1 O.R. missing	1/1
	5/6"		During the night "Y" Coy was relieved by a Coy of the 8th Bat'n LINCOLNSHIRE Reg't + rejoined the BATTALION 5/9/18. CASUALTY - 1. O.R. wounded	

Place	Date SEPT	Hour	Summary of Events and Information	Remarks and references to Appendices
CANAL N. of HAVRINCOURT WOOD	7th	7.45 p.m.	MAJOR T.J.E. BLAKE 13th ROYAL FUSILIERS took over command of the Battn from Lt. Col. A.R.C. SANDERS C.M.G. D.S.O. to 50th INF. Bde. The Battn proceeded to the relief of the 13th ROYAL FUSILIERS in front line K.25 and 32 N. of HAVRINCOURT WOOD. Relief complete 10 P.M.	APPENDIX I
"	8th		In accordance with orders received at 2.0 p.m. "Z" COY under command of Capt. W.D. MATHIESON M.C. occupied the TRENCH on YORKSHIRE BANK with No. 14. PLATOON establishing posts at K.32.a.7.8 - K.32.a.70.65, & K32.a.6.4 from this TRENCH a reconnoitring PATROL went out, proceeding along YORKSHIRE ALLEY to K.32.b.05.95. The short TRENCH running from this point N.W. to the CANAL was observed to be empty, so the PATROL worked along the TRENCH to the right. An enemy Post was encountered at K.32.b.2.7. Having gained this information, the PATROL withdrew. A Post was then established at K.32.b.05.95.	
		9.0 p.m.	Two PLATOONS of X COY were sent up as additional support and were placed in CHEETHAM SWITCH & EASTERN END of HENLEY AVENUE, when that two PLATOONS were in position, 15. PLATOON ("Z" Coy) was transferred from the WESTERN END of HENLEY AVENUE to the Dug out at K.32.0.5.9. One PLATOON from "W" COY & one PLATOON from "X" COY	

Army Form C. 2118.

WAR DIARY
or
INTELLIGENCE SUMMARY

(Erase heading not required.)

Place	Date	Hour	Summary of Events and Information	Remarks and references to Appendices
CANAL N. OF HAVRINCOURT WOOD	SEPT 8th	P.m. 9-0	were pushed forward and established Posts along the WESTERN BANK of the CANAL from RAILWAY BRIDGE K 26, central to K 31.b.1.7. CASUALTIES 3. O.Rs wounded.	nil
	9th	a.m. 9-0	The following morning a BOMBING PARTY of 6. O.Rs under CPL. WELLS was sent along the TRENCH to disperse or capture the enemy POST located the previous evening. The enemy were taken by surprise + 5 Prisoners + 1 M.G. were captured. The TRENCH having thus been cleared, No 15 PLATOON were sent up to occupy it with orders to reconnoitre the TRENCHES leading to the EASTERN EDGE of YORKSHIRE BANK. PATROLS were accordingly sent along. These two TRENCHES, but were unable to proceed more than 100 yds owing to heavy M.G. fire from the FLANKS; both TRENCHES also were very shallow and it was impossible to push further forward by daylight. PATROLS going out the LEWIS GUN POST at Previous to that K.32.a.6.3. were advanced to K.32.b.10.45, in order to cover the EASTERN EDGE of YORKSHIRE BANK and keep down enemy movement. A joint operation was then decided upon at dusk, to be carried out by "Z" COY and the two PLATOONS of "X" COY; the	

Place	Date	Hour	Summary of Events and Information	Remarks and references to Appendices
CANAL N. of HAVRINCOURT WOOD	9		objective being the SUNKEN ROAD from K.32.b.95.80. to K.32.b.54.5. + the TRENCH from K.32.b.54. to K.32.b.55.05. "Z" Coy provided 3 strong parties of 1 Sgt + 10 O.Rs each. One party to work along the NORTH side of YORKSHIRE BANK to K.32.b.5.9. One party to work along the TRENCH to K.32.b.5.7.; and the third party to work along the TRENCH to K.32.b.5.5.; here the three parties were to get in touch + then push on to the SUNKEN ROAD. The two PLATOONS of "X" Coy went to advance along the light RAILWAY. S. of YORKSHIRE BANK, to the junction of the SUNKEN ROAD and the TRENCH at K.32.b.50.45. One PLATOON to extend to the left along the road + one PLATOON to the right along the TRENCH. This operation was successfully carried out at 10·0 p.m. under the most unfavourable weather conditions, and resulted in the capture by "X" Coy of 4 PRISONERS and 1 M.G. The whole of these operations were carried out without a single casualty. Casualties 2 O.Rs wounded	
LEBUCQUIÈRE	10th	4·0 a.m 8·0 a.m	The BATTALION was relieved by the 8th Battn LINCOLNSHIRE REGT and arrived in BILLETS at LEBUCQUIÈRE at 8·0 a.m under the leadership of Capt W.D. MATHIESON, M.C.	

Army Form C. 2118.

WAR DIARY

or

~~INTELLIGENCE SUMMARY~~

(Erase heading not required.)

Instructions regarding War Diaries and Intelligence Summaries are contained in F. S. Regs., Part II. and the Staff Manual respectively. Title pages will be prepared in manuscript.

Place	Date	Hour	Summary of Events and Information	Remarks and references to Appendices
EAST OFFRE BERTINCOURT	11	5-30	The Battn moved up to positions in RAILWAY CUTTING P.2d in support to 111th Inf Bde.	APPENDIX 3
	12/13		LEWIS GUN TRAINING by Companies	APPENDIX 3
	14		"W" Coy occupied PAUPER TRENCH according to orders Casualty 2/Lt W.G. HEMMINGS (accidentally wounded)	APPENDIX 4
	15th	a.m. 7-0	"W" and "Y" Companies moved forward to SPOIL HEAP J.35 d. 0.5 and SUNKEN ROAD J.36.0.8.0 respectively	APPENDIX 5
		p.m. 8-0	The Battn moved forward and relieved the 10th Batt ROYAL FUSILIERS in the LINE in DERBY TRENCH, N.E. of TRESCAULT. Relief complete 1-0 a.m. 16/19/18. Casualties - 5. ORs wounded.	
TRESCAULT TRENCH	16th		Casualties 5 ORs wounded.	
	17th	1-30 a.m. & 6-30 a.m.	The Battn AREA was heavily shelled in an enemy C.B. between 1-30 a.m. & 6-30 a.m. Casualties - 13. ORs wounded	APPENDIX 6
RESCAULT TRENCH	18th	a.m. 5-20	"W" Coy in conjunction with the 13th Battn ROYAL FUSILIERS on the right carried out an operation against a portion of CHAPEL WOOD SWITCH and DERBY TRENCH	APPENDIX 6a & 6.b.

WAR DIARY
or
~~INTELLIGENCE SUMMARY~~

(Erase heading not required.)

Army Form C. 2118.

Place	Date	Hour	Summary of Events and Information	Remarks and references to Appendices
TRESCAULT TRENCH	SEPT 18th	5.0 p.m.	Enemy counter attacked on "Y" Coy. Front. Casualties 2/Lt F.H. MIDDLETON M.C. wounded 5.ORs Killed, 16 ORs wounded 11.ORs missing	MM
E. of VELU.	19th	10-0 p.m.	The Battn was relieved by the 8th Battn LINCOLNSHIRE Regt and arrived in Billets J.33.a.od 34. at 1-0 am 20/9/18. Casualties 1.OR. Killed 7.ORs wounded	APPENDIX 7 MM
	20th	5-0 p.m.	Inspection of ARMS + EQUIPMENT.	MM
WARLENCOURT	21st		The Battn was relieved by the 1/4th Battn MANCHESTER Regt and marched to WARLENCOURT arriving there at 10-0 pm	APPENDIX 8 MM
	22		Improvement of accomodation	MM
	23rd 24th 25th		COMPANY TRAINING.	MM

WAR DIARY
or
~~INTELLIGENCE SUMMARY.~~
(Erase heading not required.)

Army Form C. 2118.

Place	Date	Hour	Summary of Events and Information	Remarks and references to Appendices
WARLENCOURT	Sept 26th		COMPANY TRAINING. A joint Concert was given in the evening by the Battn and the 13th ROYAL FUSILIERS.	
	27th		COMPANY TRAINING	
	28th		BATTALION ROUTE MARCH	
	29th	8.30 am	The Battn marched to BEUGNY arriving 12-Noon	
BEUGNY	30th	10-0 am	The Battn proceeded by bus to S.W. corner of HAVRINCOURT WOOD debussing at 12.Noon and at 5-0 pm marched to position in Q.23. in support to the 111th INF BDE. arriving 9-0 p.m. MM	APPENDIX 9

CONFIDENTIAL

WAR DIARY

OF

1ST BN. THE ESSEX REGT

FOR THE MONTH OF

OCTOBER 1918

VOLUME 44

WAR DIARY

Army Form C. 2118.

(Erase heading not required.)

Place	Date Oct	Hour	Summary of Events and Information	Remarks and references to Appendices
SWAP RESERVE	1.		The day was spent on the improvement of TRENCH SHELTERS.	
"	2		Training under Company arrangements with special instruction and practice in the use of the German Hand Grenade	
	3/4		Batt. Training under Company arrangements	
LA VACQUERIE	5	2.0 pm	The Batt. marched to LA VACQUERIE arriving 16.00 hrs and was accommodated in TRENCH SHELTERS	APPENDIX I
	6		B.M. WARNING ORDER was received for the Batt. to be prepared to move at 18.00 hrs. Reconnoitring Parties were sent forward.	APPENDIX II
CHENEAUX WOOD	7	20.00	The Batt. moved into position in the CHENEAUX WOOD preparatory to the attack	APPENDIX III / IV
	8	01.30	The WOOD was heavily shelled causing the following casualties 6. ORs WOUNDED + 14. ORs MISSING	
		03.30	The Batn. was formed up in assembly positions X Coy on the Right with Y Coy in Support Z Coy on the LEFT with W Coy in Support	

WAR DIARY
INTELLIGENCE SUMMARY

Army Form C. 2118.

Place	Date	Hour	Summary of Events and Information	Remarks and references to Appendices
CHEAUX WOOD	8		NZs (1st Battn (Otago Rifles) on the LEFT of the Battn & the 13th Royal Fusiliers on the Right	
		05:00	The Battn moved forward to the RED LINE, passing through the 111th Inf. Bde. During this movement No 5 Platoon X Coy cleared BELL AISE FARM of the enemy, capturing 30 prisoners	
		09:02	The Battn moved forward to the attack and gained objective (GREEN LINE) at about 09-30hrs, from here success was exploited as far as GREEN DOTTED LINE where posts were established. Throughout this operation touch was kept with NZs on the LEFT & Royal Fusiliers & 11th HERTS on the RIGHT	
			Casualties:- 2/Lt. C.H. REID Killed " S.W. HUGES " " N.A. NOBLE died of wounds Lt. Col. T.J.E. BLAKE, D.S.O. wounded (remained on Duty) 2/Lt. A.H. DAVISON, wounded (on Duty) " D.W. MITCHELL " " R.P. BLACKMORE " " A.J.F. SIMS "	

WAR DIARY
or
INTELLIGENCE SUMMARY.

(Erase heading not required.)

Army Form C. 2118.

Place	Date	Hour	Summary of Events and Information	Remarks and references to Appendices
			CASUALTIES total 24 ORs KILLED 107 ORs WOUNDED 27 ORs MISSING	APPENDIX V
	9	0100	The Battn moved forward to jumping off point E of HANCOURT in order W - Z and from there advanced to the attack Y - X	AH
WEST OF CAUDRY		16:00	at 09.20 reached the Second objective 12.00 approx. The Battn advanced on CAUDRY + were held up on the line of the RAILWAY. where the Coys were reorganised and dug in CASUALTIES - 2/Lt AB CRABTREE WOUNDED C.H.J. CAUDELL	
			14 ORs WOUNDED 3 ORs MISSING	
EAST OF BETHENCOURT	10	08:30	Without ARTILLERY preparation the Battn attacked and secured CAUDRY reaching FINAL OBJECTIVE EAST OF BETHENCOURT at about 10-30 Two front line Coys W + Z dug in Y Coy withdrew to Support + dug in + X Coy was withdrawn + placed in RESERVE in the VILLAGE	APPENDIX VI
	11	18:00	The Battn marched to LIGNY and arrived in BILLETS at 20.00 hrs	

Army Form C. 2118.

WAR DIARY
or
INTELLIGENCE SUMMARY.
(Erase heading not required.)

Place	Date	Hour	Summary of Events and Information	Remarks and references to Appendices
LIGNY	Oct 12		Resting in Billets	
"	13		BATT^N CHURCH PARADE	
"	14		Training under Coy arrangements	App 3
"	15		Training under company arrangements	App 3
"	16		"	App 3
"	17		BATT^N PARADE	App 3
"	18		BATT^N PARADE for inspection by G.O.C. 112th INF BDE	App 3
"	19		Training under company arrangements	App 3
"	20		CHURCH PARADE	App 3
"	21		Training under Company arrangements. BDE warning order received, warning BATT^N to be prepared to move up forward, attached to 111th BDE	APPENDIX VII App 3

Army Form C. 2118.

WAR DIARY
or
INTELLIGENCE SUMMARY.

(Erase heading not required.)

Instructions regarding War Diaries and Intelligence Summaries are contained in F. S. Regs., Part II. and the Staff Manual respectively. Title pages will be prepared in manuscript.

Place	Date Oct	Hour	Summary of Events and Information	Remarks and references to Appendices
LIGNY	22nd	10.30 a.m.	Battalion marched to VIESLY and billeted in barns	APPENDIX VIII
VIESLY	23rd	4 a.m.	Battalion moved by columns to a position S.E. of BRIASTRE Regt S/w/ of support to the 6th WINNERS Battns suitably form T.H.Q. at E.25.a.9.5 to E.23.a.4.6. Ration & Pack Transport Battns Transport Rn THQ went to E.25.a.4.9.	
		8 a.m.	Battn moved forward to a position W. of BROWN HIVE two coys in the front line E.31.0.1.5 & E.31.c.3.5 & two coys in support about E.30.d. Bn THQ at Bn HQ at E.31.b.3.4	
W. of BRIASTRE		11.15 a.m.	Battalion moved to BLAUBAIN in rear of attacking Battns	
		2 p.m.	The attacking waves reached objectives from W. of ST. MAURICE to E.6.b.5.5 (N.E. of NEUVILLE) about 11 a.m.	
BLAUBAIN		12.04 p.m.	Orders received to attack objective N. of GREEN Line at NEUVILLE	
		1 p.m.	Coys pushed forward Battns deployed behind GREEN BATTLE line to SALISBURY & attack to be launched from GREEN BATTLE line E.11.c.	
NEUVILLE			BROWN LINE IS N.W. and W. of Quennent W. 24 & 26.	

Summary of operations from 22/10/18 to 27/10/18 attached

Army Form C. 2118.

WAR DIARY
or
INTELLIGENCE SUMMARY
(Erase heading not required)

Instructions regarding War Diaries and Intelligence Summaries are contained in F. S. Regs., Part II and the Staff Manual respectively. Title pages will be prepared in manuscript.

Place	Date	Hour	Summary of Events and Information	Remarks and references to Appendices
NEUVILLE	OCT 23rd	23.59	Bn. continued advance on BEAUTY LINE & lay on GREEN DOTTED LINE on 24th the ground from X 20.c.6.8 to X.18.c.80	
	24th	0.30	Orders received from Bde. In accordance with to trenches W of GREEN DOTTED LINE. Warning order that the battalion would make attack on to H29 Red from 0400 to 4 onwards 1128 Red from R 34 central to X 5 central	
		0.m	H23h Bn. arranged as the coming morning off at the GREEN DOTTED LINE	
		425	Winced Z continued in PRACTICE TRENCHES (W of GHISSIGNIES) & company dim to form a defensive flank along southern wall from X 20 b 4.2 to X.15.a.15. X Coy took up a position on X 13.c	
		070	C company to lay alleys and markers from Z Coy will short of PRACTICE TRENCHES to a function near X in ground a	
		1600	Bn. HQ moved to to SALESCHES	
		730	Warning Order from Brigade for Battn. to be prepared to	

Army Form C. 2118.

WAR DIARY
or
INTELLIGENCE SUMMARY
(Erase heading not required.)

Instructions regarding War Diaries and Intelligence Summaries are contained in F. S. Regs., Part II. and the Staff Manual respectively. Title pages will be prepared in manuscript.

Place	Date	Hour	Summary of Events and Information	Remarks and references to Appendices
SALESCHES	24/10/18	19:30	Relieved the 13th R.F. in left of Brigade front after a minor operation to be reversed on line of 13th R.F. on left and 1/1 Herts on right	Ay3
		21:00	Three operations to make good the front of main from P.36 central 16 × 5 central and then stood by ready to move on	
			Later returned to staff of 13th R.F. until	APPENDIX IX
	25/10/18	04:05	Battalion relieved Batt. of 13th R.F. on Rds Jn X.15.C.6.7 to X.15.d.2.9. h to be ready to move	
		07:30	Battalion moved up to relieve 13th R.F. of 6 MISSING.35	
		21:00	W Coy left front Z Coy right front Y Coy in reserve X Coy	
		23:00	Coy positions were unknown and heavily shelled causing many casualties	
			Killed O/R **Wounded** 7 O/R	
		23:55	Relief reported complete	

Army Form C. 2118.

WAR DIARY
or
INTELLIGENCE SUMMARY.
(Erase heading not required.)

Instructions regarding War Diaries and Intelligence Summaries are contained in F. S. Regs., Part II. and the Staff Manual respectively. Title pages will be prepared in manuscript.

Place	Date	Hours	Summary of Events and Information	Remarks and references to Appendices
GHISSIGNIES	24/10/18		The men suffered by the battalion was heavy. Allied with H.E. and gas during the day, causing about 16 gas casualties.	
	27/10/18	15.00	Warning order received.	
		17.30	Battalion was relieved by 5th Somerset L.I.	
		19.50	Relief reported complete. Bn. moved by companies to VITER-LANTARD — SALESCHES.	MB
VITER-LAN	28/10/18	13.00	Three companies rested during morning. Battalion moved further back to billets in BEAURAIN	APPENDIX X
BEAURAIN.	29/10/18 30/10/18 31/10/18		} Training under Company arrangements	MB

Murrel Welch
LT.-COLONEL
COMDG. 1st BN. THE ESSEX REGT.

1ST BATTN THE ESSEX REGIMENT

SUMMARY OF OPERATIONS from 22/10/18 to 27/10/18

On Tuesday 22nd October 1918 the battalion was attached to the 111th Brigade for an Operation to be carried out on Wednesday 23rd October. At 1030 hours the battalion marched from LIGNY to VIESLY, being accommodated in billets there. A reconnaissance was carried out on the afternoon of the 22nd of the approaches to the river and railway S.E. of BRIASTRE.

At 0400 hours 23rd October the battalion moved up by Companies to positions in E.25. Two Companies (W & Z) on line of railway from E.25.a.9.8. to E.25.d.3.9. and two companies in the practice trenches in E.25.a. Battalion Hq. at E.25.c.5.8. The 10th R.Fs. were on our right.

At 0800 hours, in accordance with instructions contained in Operation orders, the battalion moved forward to occupy an area West of BEAURAIN.

At 0845 hours it was found that the 5th Division had failed to establish their line and consequently the 13th Bn. Rifle Brigade, to which this battalion was in support, had not moved forward. The battalion accordingly took up defensive positions and dug in. Two companies along bank from E.15.d.1.7. to E.21.b.3.6. and two companies on road from E.15.c.7.9. to E.15.c.1.8. Battalion Hqs. was established at E.21.b.5. The 111th Brigade was informed of fresh dispositions and situation. Touch was later established with the 10th R.Fs. on our right.

At 1115 hours the battalion moved forward again to a position West of BEAURAIN, all companies being in E.10.d. Battalion Hqs. at E.11.a.4.5. Later at 1400 hours two companies were sent to line of railway from W.29.d.8.1. to E.6.b.9.5, the remaining two companies being in support positions in E.6.a.

About 1530 hours orders were received for the Battalion to form up at 1715 hours with the 10th R.Fs. on right preparatorily to attacking the green dotted and brown lines. under a barrage. orders were accordingly issued for the battalion to form up on the road running S.E. from W.30.a. to X.25.c. Battalion Hqs. was established at ST.MORRIS'S CHAPEL. At 1711 hours Zero hour was altered to 1730 hours and companies informed. At 1718 hours orders were received by telephone that the attack was to take place without a barrage. The forward move was consequently stopped and the situation explained fully to all company Commanders. Battalion Hqs. was established at W.24.d.20. and Brigade informed.

At 1740 hours companies moved off. Y. company moved straight into the village to make good all exits and to mop up. W & Z companies moved forward with instruction to establish the GREEN DOTTED line and push forward from there to the BROWN LINE. These companies moved by platoons in Echelon West of the village.

W & Z companies pushed forward to the GREEN DOTTED LINE avoiding the villages of NEUVILLE and SALESCHES as far as possible. Y. company made good the villages. X. company was kept in reserve.

Having secured the GREEN DOTTED LINE W & Z companies pushed on to the BROWN LINE while Y. company established posts on the GREEN DOTTED LINE about midnight 23rd. No opposition was encountered but forward companies experienced the greatest difficulty in getting forward owing to the darkness of the night and the very thick under growth which had in places to be hacked away. All crossings of the river were made good and the northern bank was secured by the mopping up company. X.company took up a position in road from FERME BERNIER to cross roads at X.20.c 9.9. Touch was maintained with the New Zealand Brigade on our left throughout the whole of the operations.

About 0300 hours orders were received that from 0400 hours onwards the battalion would revert to 112th Brigade and information was received that the 112th Brigade would attack at 0400 hours and capture GHISSIGNIES and sunken road from R.34.c.8.9. to X.5.a.2.9. and secure the line of railway from X.5.a.2.9. to X.5.c.6.0.

In accordance with instructions ~~with instructions~~ received companies were ordered to withdraw to positions behind the GREEN DOTTED LINE, to allow the 13th R.Fs. with 1/1st Herts operating on their right, to go through and capture the above objectives. This was done and at 0400 hours the attack was launched. At about 0600 hours the Battalion was ordered forward to support the 13th R.Fs. W & Z Companies took up a position in PRACTICE TRENCHES, but owing to heavy M.G. fire from the right Z company was withdrawn to a position in X.14.g. About 0825 hours Y.company was sent to form a defensive flank along sunken road from X.20.b.4.2. to X.21.a.6.9. while X.company took up a supporting position in X.15.c.

A warning order was received from Brigade about 1700 hours for the Battalion to be prepared to relieve the 13th R.Fs. that evening. This order was cancelled about 0400 Hours on 25th.

The dispositions of the battalion were maintained as above until the evening of the 25th when the battalion moved forward to relieve the 13th R.Fs. on left sector of Brigade front North of GHISSIGNIES. W & Z companys took over the outpost line consisting of pests along sunken road from R.34.c.7.9. to X.5.a.2.8. Y.company took up a support position along road from X.3.b.7.8. to X.4.a.70.05. and X.company was in reserve about X.4.c.6.8.

Y.company was heavily shelled with H.E. and Gas soon after taking up their position, several casualties being inflicted.

The Battalion held the line until the evening of the 27th being subjected during this period to heavy shelling from High explosive and Gas shells. On 27th the battalion was relieved by 8th Somerset Light Infantry. Relieve was completed by 1930 hours and battalion was back to Billets VITERLAN and SALESCHES by 2100 hours.

29/10/18.

Terence Blake
Lieut Col.
Commdg 1st Battn the Essex Regiment.

Confidential

War Diary

of

1ˢᵗ Battn. The Essex Regᵗ

for

November 1918

Volume 45

Army Form C. 2118.

WAR DIARY

(Erase heading not required.)

Place	Date	Hour	Summary of Events and Information	Remarks and references to Appendices
BEAURAIN	1/11/18		Range was allotted to W and Y Coys. Other Companies instructed routine Ordinary Conversation arrangements.	
	2/11/18		Primordies under Coy arrangements. 2 Lewis Guns and S.A.A. Battalion fitted	worn
	3/11/18		Battalion moved to SALESCHES preliminary to awaiting the attack, & remained in billets for the night. In the early morning the Village was shelled causing the following casualties. 10 O.R. killed 22 O.R. wounded	APPENDIX I + II
				worn
	4/11/18		Battn. moved from SALESCHES about 0630 hrs to GHISSIGNIES. Battn. attacked & reached final objective E of JOLIMETZ about 1500 hrs.	APPENDIX III
			2nd Lt R.L. Tourret wounded & remained on duty. 3 O.R. killed 18 O.R. wounded	worn
	5/11/18		At 10.00 hrs battalion marched to billets in GHISSIGNIES, remaining until about 14.00 hrs.	worn

Army Form C. 2118.

WAR DIARY

or ~~INTELLIGENCE SUMMARY~~.

(Erase heading not required.)

Instructions regarding War Diaries and Intelligence Summaries are contained in F. S. Regs., Part II. and the Staff Manual respectively. Title pages will be prepared in manuscript.

Place	Date	Hour	Summary of Events and Information	Remarks and references to Appendices
GUSSIGNIES	1/1/18		Battalion rested	
"	2/1/18		Reorganisation of Companies & attachments of stores.	WBM
"	3/1/18		Parades under Company arrangements	WBM
"	4/1/18		Two Companies under Coy arrangements. No trap in afternoon owing to C.O. visit	WBM
"	5/1/18		On 1050 hrs. Battalion Church Parade	WBM
"	6/1/18		Battn. marched from GUSSIGNIES to billets in BETHENCOURT arriving 1545 hrs.	WBM
BETHENCOURT	7/1/18		Inspection of all Coys arms equipment clothing & necessaries. Battn. Commanders Conference	WBM
"	8/1/18		Presentation of medals & parades under Coy arrangements. Battn. killed by Cambrai. Battn. containing football comp.	WBM
"	9/1/18			
"	10/1/18		Two Coys allotted range & Fire trap close order drill. Parades under Coy arrangements	WBM
"	11/1/18		Divisional Church Parade.	WBM

Army Form C. 2118.

WAR DIARY
or
~~INTELLIGENCE SUMMARY.~~

(Erase heading not required.)

Instructions regarding War Diaries and Intelligence Summaries are contained in F. S. Regs., Part II. and the Staff Manual respectively. Title pages will be prepared in manuscript.

Place	Date	Hour	Summary of Events and Information	Remarks and references to Appendices
BATHENCOURT	13/11/18		Brigade Sports 1st Essex won Challenge Cup	WDMM
	14/11/18		Battalion lectures instruction to General Commanders in situation held in theatre at CAVORY by General	
			Education Officer - Subjects Demobilisation	WDMM
	21/11/18		Brigade inspection Major H E Horsfield M.C., RE hosted as	
			Attend in command from 18th 11.18	WDMM
	22/11/18		At 1000 hrs General Commanders inspection	WDMM
			Parades under Coy arrangements	WDMM
	23/11/18		Billes instruction by Commanding Officer	WDMM
	24/11/18		Church Parade at 1045 hrs	WDMM
			Parades under Coy arrangements	WDMM
	26/11/18		Brigade Route march at 0900 hrs	WDMM
	27/11/18		Major Horsfield M.C. takes over command of battalion	
			during absence of Lt col T J E Blake D.S.O. on leave.	WDMM
	28/11/18		Range allotted to W Coy from 9 Y lay instructed by	
			Armament Sergeant this Coy handed under Coy arrangements.	WDMM

Army Form C. 2118.

WAR DIARY
or
~~INTELLIGENCE SUMMARY~~

(Erase heading not required.)

Instructions regarding War Diaries and Intelligence Summaries are contained in F. S. Regs., Part II. and the Staff Manual respectively. Title pages will be prepared in manuscript.

Place	Date	Hour	Summary of Events and Information	Remarks and references to Appendices
BETH ENCOURT	30/1/18		Got 1600 tons teak wood saw for B Battn Sports	APPENDIX IV
	31/1/18		Battn. Sports at 1030 hrs	
	1/2/18			

APPENDIX I

1ST ESSEX REGT. - OPERATION ORDER No.71.

Ref Maps.
51A.S.W.
51.S.W.
1/20,000

Copy No. 11

1. The 112th Inf. Bde., plus 8th Somerset Light Infantry, will move on 3rd November to area of GHISSIGNIES.
   112th Inf. Bde. Hqrs. will close at BEAURAIN at 2000 hrs. and re-open at X.4.c.8.6. (GHISSIGNIES) on arrival.

2. The 1st. Bn. Essex Regt. will move to PRACTICE TRENCHES X.9.a. & b. and NORTH of D. Battn Hq. will be established at X.8.b.2.2. approx.

3. The march will be by platoons at 50 yards distance.
   Order of March: "X" "Y" "Z" "B.H.Q."
   Dress: Marching Order: Packs slung.
   Route: Right Fork at fork roads E.11.b.5.6. N.N.E. to E.6.a.7.8. thence S.E. to F.1.c.8.0. NORTHERLY direction through NEUVILLE - SALESCHES to FARM BERRIER thence by track.
   Starting point: Fork roads E.11.b.5.6.

4. The head of "X" Coy. will pass the starting point at 1550 hrs.

5. Lewis Gun Limbers (1 per company and 1 for B.H.Q.) will report to companies at 1545 hrs. and will accompany their respective companies returning to Transport lines when unloaded.
   Two cookers and 1 Water Cart will follow the Battalion. The cookers will provide Breakfast for the battalion and will return to Transport Lines at first opportunity after the Battalion has moved forward.

6. All Battle stores and rations for the 4th (with exception of Breakfast Ration which will be on cookers) will be issued before leaving BEAURAIN.

7. 1 N.C.O. per company, as a Forward party will report to Lt. Dickinson at Battn. Orderly Room at 1330 hrs. this party will avoid movement on high ground.

8. Arrival in new position will be notified by runner to Battn Hqrs.

9. 1 Drummer per company and B.H.Q. will be detailed as guard over dumps.

10. Breakfast will be eaten at PRACTICE TRENCHES on the morning of Novr. 4th at 0430 hrs.

11. Officers' valises and Men's blankets will be dumped at Quartermasters Stores by 1800 hrs.

2/11/18.

H.Daly
Captain & A/Adjt.
1st Battn. The Essex Regiment.

Distribution
Copy No.1. - 112th Inf. Bde.   Copy No. 9. - 15th R.Fs.
"   " 2. - C.O.   "   "   10. - R.S.M.
"   " 3. - "Y" Coy.   "   "   11. - War Diary
"   " 4. - "X" "   "   "   12. -
"   " 5. - "Z" "   "   "   13. - File.
"   " 6. - "Z" "
"   " 7. - Q.M.
"   " 8. - T.O.

1st. BATTN. THE ESSEX REGIMENT.

Amendment to Operation Order No. 71.

Para. 1. For Area of GHISSIGNIES read area of just EAST of F.M. BERNIER X 20 a.

Para 2. Cancel and substitute: "1st Bn Essex Regt will move to area just east of B FM. BERNIER X 20 a 08 . The Battn. Hd.Qrs. will be established at, or in the vicinity of FM Bernier.

Para 3. Route will be the same as far as FM BERNIER.

Para 4. For 1630 hrs, read 1700 hrs.

Para 5. Add "1 pack animal will accompany each Coy, and carry L.G. magazines from FM BERNIER as far as the tactical situation admits.

ADDITION. Watches will be synchronised at Battn. Hd. Qrs. at 2115 hrs. 3rd. instant.

3rd Novr./18.

H Daly
Captain & Adjutant,
1st. Bn. The Essex Regiment.

Distribution:-

    Copy No. 1   112th. Infy Bde.
     "   "   2   C.O.
     "   "   3   "W" Coy.
     "   "   4   "X" Coy.
     "   "   5   "Y" Coy.
     "   "   6   "Z" Coy.
     "   "   7   Q.M.
     "   "   8   T.O.
     "   "   9   13th R.F.
     "   "   10   R.S.M.
     "   "   11)
     "   "   12) War Diary.
     "   "   13. File.

APPENDIX II

1st ESSEX OPERATION ORDER NO. 72.

Copy No.

Ref Maps
51 A S.E
51 S.W

1. The advance will be resumed on the early morning of the 4th November.

2. The 17th Div. will be attacking on the right, and the N.Z. Div. on the left of the 37th Div. The N.Z. Div. are not attacking the town of LE QUESNOY, but encircling it from the North & South, their two attacking columns gaining touch on the GREEN LINE.

3. The 111th. Infantry Brigade will capture the BLUE and DOTTED BLUE LINES. The 112th Infantry Brigade will pass through the 111th Infantry Brigade on the DOTTED BLUE LINE, and will capture the GREEN RED & BROWN LINE, and will exploit success to the DOTTED RED LINE.

4. The attack will be carried out under an Artillery, T.M. & M.G. Barrage. The artillery barrage will open on BLACK LINE at ZERO.
   The Artillery Barrage will leave
   BLACK LINE at ZERO plus 4 minutes.
   BLUE LINE at " " 119 "
   DOTTED BLUE LINE " " 197 "
   GREEN LINE for attack on RED LINE at ZERO plus 342 min.
   " " " " " BROWN LINE " " 449 "

5. The following pauses will be made in the barrage
   On BLUE LINE 15 minutes.
   On DOTTED BLUE LINE 30 minutes.
   On GREEN LINE (on left) 12 minutes.
   On GREEN LINE (on right) 2 hours.

6. The Barrage will creep forward at a uniform rate of a 100 yards in six minutes except that
   (a) The advance from the GREEN to the RED LINE will be a 100 yds. in 4 minutes.

7. <u>INTENTION</u>. This Battalion will take part in a Brigade attack.
   Battalion objective - the RED & BROWN LINES.
   The 1/1 Herts. are attacking on the right.

8. INTER-DIVISIONAL & BATTALION BOUNDARIES ETC are as per attached tracing.
   INTER-COMPANY BOUNDARIES.
   <u>Inclusive to "Z" Company</u>. Farm de l' Hopital - Track & Road Junction S.4.a.30.10.- Road Junction S.5.b.75.20 (=liason (liaison post with "Y" Company)
   <u>INCLUSIVE to "Y" Company</u>. - CHATEAU in S.4.a.- Road running East in S.4.a & b - to a point on the road in S.5.b 400 yards s. of Bridge in M.35.c.

9. The Battalion will assemble for attack on the DOTTED BLUE LINE, and will advance at ZERO plus 197 minutes.
   The Battalion will form up on the DOTTED BLUE LINE as follows;
   "Z" Company Right Company.
   "Y" " Centre "
   "X" " Left "
   "W" " Support. "

10. "W" Company will be in support, and will follow the Right Company at a distance of 250 yards. This Company will mop up the village of JOLIMETZ, and will detail platoons to certain areas as arranged at conference. A Platoon will be kept in reserve in the neighbourhood of the CHURCH at JOLIMETZ.

Page 2.

11. Liaison posts will be established as follows:-
   With N.Z. at Road Junction M.34.c.9.7.   "X" Company,
   "   "   "   "   M.36.c.1.7.   "X"   "
   "   1/1st Herts at CHURCH JOLIMETZ   "W"   "
   "   "   "   " ROAD JUNCTION S.5.c.8.1   "Z"   "
   "   Inter Company S.5.b.75.20.   "Z" & "Y" Coys.

12. The Objective once gained will be held at all costs.
    Companies will at once re-organize in depth, and dig in.
    Every effort must be made to keep direction, and advantage taken during the advance of the natural features to re-organize the line and press forward. After the objective has been gained, the 13th Royal Fusiliers will pass through and capture the DOTTED RED LINE. "X" & "Y" Coys. will then push L.G. posts on the road, and will occupy posts at M.36.c.65.20.- S.6.a.20.65. - S.5.b.70.20.

13. AID POST. Farm de l'HOPITAL till GREEN LINE is captured: after CHURCH JOLIMETZ.

14. Prisoners ......ditto......ditto......

15. COMMUNICATION The S.O. will arrange for a wire to be laid from FARM de l'HOPITAL to CHATEAU in S.4.a. From there a line will be laid to a point on the Railway approx. M.35.d.4.0. All Coys. should be able to tap in on this line.

16. TRANSPORT. As the intention is for the 5th Div. To relieve the 37th Div. as soon as objectives have been gained, the T.O. will detail five limbers to be in the vicinity of CHURCH JOLIMETZ at 1300 hrs. These will be used to carry back Lewis Guns etc. All other Transport will be dealt with as per Brigade Administrative Instructions in possession of T.O. The Tool Limber will move with Echelon "A".

17. REPORTS. To Farm de l'HOPITAL till GREEN LINE is made good; after that to CHATEAU in S.4.a.

18.   ZERO   0530 hrs.

19. MACHINE GUN. A Section of M.G.'s will be with the Battalion, and will continue the advance with the 13th R.F.

20. TRENCH MORTAR. 1, T.M. will be with the Battalion, and will continue the advance with the R 13th. R.F.

21. TANKS. Five Tanks, Mk.V, of "C"Coy, No. 14 Tank Battn. will assist in the attack on JOLIMETZ, and the RED LINE.

22. COMPASS BEARING. The general compass bearing of the attack is 102 degrees MAGNETIC.

23. CONTACT AEROPLANE. A Contact Aeroplane will call for flares at   ZERO plus 110.
                        ZERO " 170.
                         "   " 270.
   - And at intervals of 2 hrs. afterwards. In thick woods flares will be lit in rides and clearings.

                                          Lieut-Colonel,
                                    Cmmdg, 1st. Bn. The Essex Regt.

APPENDIX III

1ST BATTN THE ESSEX REGIMENT.

SUMMARY OF OPERATIONS FROM NOVR. 3rd - NOVR 5th 1918.

November 3rd
On November 3rd about 1700 hours the battalion marched from BEAURAIN to SALESCHES where it billetted for the night.
The village was shelled intermittingly during the night and one shell struck the barn in which "Y" Company was billetted and Killed One and wounded 21 O.Rs. a platoon of the reserve company ("W" Coy) was consequently attached to "Y" Company for the forthcoming operations.

November 4th
At 0600 hours in accordance with orders the battalion moved off from SALESCHES by platoons at 100 yards distance. Pack animals accompanied companies, carrying the Lewis Gun Ammunition as far as Ghissignies, Route. FME BERNIER - BANDAG TRACK - SUNKEN ROAD X.4.a. & b. - The battalion had been organised for the attack as follows:-

Right Front Coy	Centre Coy.	Left front Coy.
"Z" Coy	(with 1. T.M. attached)	"X" Coy
CAPT WALKER	"Y" Coy	CAPTAIN CALVERLEY M.C.
	CAPT ATTFIELD	

Reserve Coy. "W" Coy. - CAPT. GILLETT

A Cavalry patrol consisting of 1 Officer and 5 troopers were attached also a section of Machine Guns. Both of these were told to Rendezvous at FME. DE. L'HOPITAL at 0915 hours, if the tactical situation permitted.
Each Company was to advance on a two platoon front with one platoon in support. The Reserve Company was to mop up the village of JOLIMETZ and leave a permanent garrison in same.
The battalion arrived in Sunken road X.4.a. & b. without incident at 0645 hours. It was found on arrival that the left of the 13th Rifle Brigade had not been able to proceed as the enemy holding the railway and CHAPEL, had not been cleared. This was communicated to Brigade and the battalion was ordered to stand by for further orders and push patrols out to get in touch and observation in front. It was later established that the Right company of the 13th Rifle Brigade had pushed on and orders were accordingly issued to "Z" (Right) Coy. to push forward with all speed avoiding the CHAPEL and to make headways towards the BLUE LINE where it was hoped it would be able to reorganise and press forward "Y" (Centre) Company was ordered to push forward echelonsed to the left rear of "Z" Company and to keep in touch. "Z" Company moved off immediately on receipt of orders at 0815 hours and "Y" company followed. Messages were then received from patrols that a Tank was in action against the CHAPEL and the enemy resistance was weakening and on this information orders were eximmediately ordered to "X" (Left) Company to push forward at once on the original line of advance. The whole battalion was En route by 0840 hours.
It was found on arrival at RAILWAY in X.5.c. that the 13th Royal Fusiliers were in front of this battalion and after conference with Commanding Officer, 13th Royal Fusiliers the battalion moved through them.
From 0930 hours onwards the advance was pressed forward with the greatest rapidity. The line of advance was due E. from the cross roads in R.34.d. which enabled the battalion to be well clear of LOUVIGNIES which was under heavy shell fire. The battalion moved across the main road in LOUVIGNIES in good style but no touch could be established with any troops in front or right flank. Touch was made with the New Zealanders here and from that time never lost. The battalion came under M/G fire from direction of LE QUESNOY on the road but the fire was ill directed and no casualties occurred.
Battalion Headquarters was temporarily established at M.31.d.70. Efforts were made to get in touch on the right, the attached cavalry being fully used (and doing very excellent work) but no troops could be found. The battalion was reorganised on this line and direction and Company frontage checked. (JOLIMETZ CHURCH was now visible the smoke having cleared)

The advance was continued with the left company leading (in touch with New Zealanders) and the Centre and Right Company echeloned back as flank protection. The Right Company also had two platoons echeloned in the right rear to guard the unprotected flank and special instructions were given to the Reserve company re-same. At 1015 hours or 90 minutes behind time the whole battalion had moved across the BLUE DOTTED LINE and at 1035 hours the battalion was across the RAU DE PONT À'VACHE with orders to get across the BLUE LINE as quickly as possible and take advantage of the dis-organisation of the enemy caused by the barrage. Battalion Headquarters established at FME DE L'HOPITAL. It was here that touch was established with the 13th Rifle Brigade and elements of the Right Support Company of the 1/1 HERTS. Our dispositions and intentions were explained to the Officer in charge of the HERTS and he was asked to report same to his Commanding Officer.

The left front Company in the meantime had pushed on rapidly and by 1050 hours were well EAST of the CEMETARY (M.33.d.) The enemy appeared to be recovering from the effects of our barrage and were manning the orchards and houses and also the roads leading from JOLIMETZ. By very careful manoeuving however and by the speed of the advance the whole of the left flank of JOLIMETZ was turned and many prisoners and guns were taken. The remainder of the enemy fled into the village and were either shot or taken prisoners by the Centre company which had arrived. Both these Companies then pressed forward to the BLUE LINE and the enemy were pressed back in a S.E. direction the area S.4.d. being full of them. It was apparent that the retiring enemy had been halted and that some attempt at reorganisation was taking place. Groups of men were seen to be taking up positions in the hedges and roads in the immediate vicinity of the CHURCH and fire was opened by them at the Two companies which were pressing forward to the BLUE LINE.

At.1110 hours however the right front Company arrived and the enemy who had come under enfilade reverse (from "X" & "Y") and frontal fire came out and surrendered freely not before however a certain number had been shot or bayonetted.

The whole of the front companies were then pressed forward to the BLUE LINE and the remainder of the mopping up of the village was left in the hands of the Reserve company. Quite a deal of opposition was met with in and about the village but the hostile fire although heavy was extraordinarily wild and ineffective. It was at this juncture that a Tank (JOB 2/Lt.HARRIS) arrived on the scene and did very excellant work indeed.

Each platoon (and practically each section) of the Reserve Company had been given definite areas to mop up with the consequence that the village was cleared of the enemy in a remarkably short and thoroughly workmanlike style. Those who came out at once were taken prisoners, those who did not were shot or bayonetted. There were many wounded in the cellars who had apparently only just been dressed. These were sent down. During the whole of these operations a pocket of the enemy had been holding out in S.3.b.9.7. and fire was also being directed from the high ground S.10.b.

The two platoons of the right company detailed for flank defence took this post in hand and the T.M.BTY, attached to the Rifle Brigade was requisitioned. A platoon of the reserve company came back from JOLIMETZ and took the post in rear and by concerted action the post was rushed and the garrison (with the exception of the sniper who shot two of our men) taken prisoners. The reserve company was then ordered to gain touch on the right if possible and to take up the defensive positions in the village as arranged at the conference on 3rd inst. A platoon was sent down to the SOUTH exits of the Village as the situation on the right still remained obscure and this platoon came under very heavy fire from high ground in S.10.b. and from the houses but made excellant progress with very few casualties. The enemy were turned out of the cellars in large numbers and sent back with and without escort. Touch was established at a point on the road 100 yards NORTH of cross roads in S.17.a. with the Division on the right. Here a Brigade Major (17th Division) asked for touch to be maintained, but this could not be done as our own flank was still more or less unprotected and the platoon in question too faraway from the Main Body but it was guaranteed that the intervening area would be mopped up. The platoon then withdrew and on the way back were able to bring fire to bear on the enemy in S.10.a. who were retiring in front of the 1/1 HERTS and again a great many prisoners were taken. The enemy at this period did not appear to have much idea as to what was going on and were so bewildered that on all sides they threw down their rifles and equipment and surrendered. In all the reserve Company claim 400 prisoners. Acting on information from the civilians the CHURCH was searched. An Observation post and Machine Gun post was found in the steeple but no garrison. This post had evidently been used by the Artillery as telephone wires and switchboard were found. The body of Church was used as a hospital. In the meantime the forward Companies had pressed forward meeting with only feeble resistance. The enemy (although in large numbers and plentifully supplied with Machine Guns) did not appear to know where to fire and his flanks were being continually turned.

Battalion Headquarters JOLIMETZ CHATEAU.

At 1215 hours it was reported that an officer and three men of the Centre company were on the final objective and at 1230 the whole of the left company arrived and consolidated.

The RED LINE was definitely made good at 1300 hours with the right flank _refused_ and with a post thrown forward to the BROWN LINE on right. Patrols were pushed out as far as possible (in one case to S.6.a.25) but these were withdrawn to conform to the protective barrage. The posts on BROWN LINE were withdrawn as Right flank was still in air (These posts were reestablished at 1650 hours a Company of the 1/1 HERTS having reported in the meantime to the Company Commander of the Right Company)

The whole front was then reorganised in depth and fresh dispositions made.

Every use was made of the houses in LE ROND QUESNE for L/G positions and many excellent targets (enemy retiring across front) at short range were taken on with good results as subsequent inspection proved. Lewis Gun posts were pushed out as previously arranged to cover the rides through the Forest directly the 13th Royal Fusiliers had gone through The outpost line was reorganised for night operations and sentry groups placed.

The amount of prisoners guns etc. taken by the battalion during this operation can only be approximate as many prisoners were sent down without escort or were used for carrying casualties (our own and the enemy) and the guns may have been by now already removed.

The estimated captures are as follows:- and include a good amount of material not specified:-

          Prisoners   850 (including 1 Battalion Commander)
          Guns   19.
          M/G   60
          T.M.   25
          Limbers etc. 5.
          Horses.   18.

If the battalion had arrived only 15 minutes earlier the whole of a Red Cross personnel would have fallen into our hands.

1. The success of this operation was due to a thorough and complete understanding on the part of all ranks of the object and intention in view. All orders were, even under most difficult circumstances, readily assumilated and carried out and the battalion, despite the initial start arrived on its objective in the proper place at the right time. Company Commanders appreciated the various tactical situations with commendable accuracy and their many reports proved invaluable to the Battalion Commander. Platoon Commanders _fought_ their platoons well and displayed the greatest keenness and it was due to them that each man went into action knowing well where he had to go and what was expected from him at deiiferent places.

2. The cavalry patrol took an active part in the operations displaying the greatest keenness and intelligence, Without their very efficient cooperation it would have been difficult to have maintained control.

3. The M/G section although not brought into action with this battalion arrived at its appointed place to time despite the very heavy barrage that was put down on all well defined avenues of approach.

4. The Liaison with the R.F.A. throughout was consistently good. Major THORNE ("B" Battery 123 Bde) was always on the spot and his knowledge of the situation and his readiness to bring up his guns gave an added sense of security. The T.M. (Lt. HARDY) attached to "Y" Coy. was always in the forefront of the attack and did excellant work.

7/11/18.

Commdg 1st Battn the Essex Regiment.

Lieut Col.

APPENDIX IV

1st ESSEX OPERATION ORDER NO 75

Copy No. 11

30/11/18

REF SHEET
VALENCIENNES
1/100,000

1. (a) The Brigade will move on the 1st proximo to ST. MARTIN area.

   (b) The battalion will move and be billetted at BERMERAIN for the night 1/2nd December. Route- Road Junction 200 yards South of the second T. in BETHENCOURT; BRIASTRE; SOLESMES; MAISON BLEUE.

2. The battalion will parade on Battalion Parade Ground near Battn. H.Q. ready to move off at 0800 hours. Markers will report to R.S.M. on the ground at 0745 hours.
   Dress: Full Marching Order. Steel Helmets will be carried behind the pack. Small Box Respirators will be worn. Jerkins will be carried in the pack.

3. The following distances will be maintained on the march:-
   500 yards between Battalions
   100   "   "   Companies
   100   "   "   Units and its Transport
   50   "   "   Every 12 Vehicles

4. All Officers Kits will be taken to Q.M.Stores by 0700 hours Blankets, in bundles of 10, to be at Q.M.Stores by 0630 hours. Officers Mess Stores to be ready for loading at Company messes at 0730 hours.
   Only 2 mess boxes per company will be carried on the Mess Cart.

5. Reveille   -   0600 Hours
   Breakfast   -   0645   "
   Sick   -   0630   "
   Dinners on arrival at BERMERIAN.

6. Guides   Guides will meet the battalion at the Cross roads 100 yards South of the S. in ST. MARTIN at 1200 hrs. to guide the battalion to their billets.

7. The 50th Field Ambulance will move in rear of the Brigade column and will pick up stragglers.

8. Lt. C.P.Lawson and 1 Sergt and 3 other ranks from "X" Coy., will march in rear of the battalion to collect stragglers.

9. No man is to go to the Field Ambulance without leave from the Medical Officer.
   No man is to fall out on the line of march without a written chit from an Officer.

10. Acknowledge.

Issued at 1930 hrs.

J.H.Mackay Paxton
Capt. & Adjt.
1st Battn. The Essex Regt.

Distribution
   No. 1. - C.O.   No. 8. T.O.
    " 2. - "W" Coy   " 9. M.O.
    " 3. - "X" "   " 10. R.S.M
    " 4. - "Y" "   " 11. War Diary
    " 5. - "Z" "   " 12. "   "
    " 6. - 112th Bde   " 13. File
    " 7. - Q.M.

CONFIDENTIAL

War Diary

of

1st Battn. The Essex Regt

For the month of

December 1918

Volume 46

WAR DIARY

~~INTELLIGENCE SUMMARY~~

(Erase heading not required.)

Army Form C. 2118.

Place	Date	Hour	Summary of Events and Information	Remarks and references to Appendices
	Dec			
BETHENCOURT	1	08-12	The Battⁿ L/t BETHENCOURT by march Route to BERMERAIN arriving 1300 hrs. Remained here the night in Billetts	Appendix 1 WDM
BERMERAIN	2	0830	The Battⁿ marched from BERMERAIN to WARGNIES-le-GRAND arriving 1230 hrs. The Battⁿ was accommodated in Billets.	WDM
WARGNIES LE GRAND	3		Inspection of Billets. 1 percentage of the Battⁿ paraded with the 112th Bde Group to line the Road whilst the King passed.	WDM
"	4		Educational Classes.	WDM
"	5		Battⁿ Parade - Educational Classes	WDM
"	6		All Ranks except C.Q.M.S. - R.Q.M.S. Parade for instruction under R.S.M. - Pour Salvage Work carried out - Baths -	WDM
"	7	1000	Educational Classes Inspection of Billets by C.O. - Educational Classes	WDM
"	8		Battⁿ Church Parade	WDM
"	9		Educational Classes - Court of Inquiry re loss of 2 Bicycles	WDM

Army Form C. 2118.

WAR DIARY / INTELLIGENCE SUMMARY

(Erase heading not required.)

Instructions regarding War Diaries and Intelligence Summaries are contained in F.S. Regs., Part II. and the Staff Manual respectively. Title pages will be prepared in manuscript.

Place	Date	Hour	Summary of Events and Information	Remarks and references to Appendices
WARGNIES LE GRAND	Dec 10	—	Educational Classes	—
"	11		Battⁿ Route March to ST SAULVE	—
"	12		BRIGADE OPERATIONS	appendix IV
"	13		Educational Classes	—
"	14	1150	The Battⁿ marched from WARGNIES to BELLIGNIES arriving 1445hrs	—
"	15	1335	The Battⁿ marched from BELLIGNIES to NEUF MESNIL arriving 1800 hrs. The Battⁿ was held up at BAVAI from 1430hrs until 1535hrs to let Artillery pass	appendix IV
NEUF MESNIL	16		Colour Party arrived from England	—
"	17	1010	The Battⁿ Left NEUF MESNIL for MAIRIEUX arrived 1220 hrs	appendix V
MAIRIEUX	18	0936	The Battⁿ marched from MAIRIEUX to BINCHE arrived 1430 hrs	appendix VI
BINCHE	19	0010	" " BINCHE to TRAZEGNIES arrived 14.20 hrs	appendix VII
TRAZEGNIES	20	0915	" " TRAZEGNIES to RANSART arrived 1430 hrs	appendix VIII
RANSART	21		The Battⁿ Rested - accommodated in Billets	—
"	22		Battⁿ Church Parade	—

WAR DIARY
INTELLIGENCE SUMMARY
(Erase heading not required.)

Army Form C. 2118.

Place	Date	Hour	Summary of Events and Information	Remarks and references to Appendices
RANSART	DEC 23		The Battn Batted	
"	24		Parades under Company Arrangements	
"	25		Voluntary Church Service	
"	26		General Routine	
"	27	noon	General Reuters [?]	
"	28		Educational Classes	
"	29		Battn Church Parade — Educational Classes	
"	30		The first performance of The Flat Irons Concert Party	
"	31		C.C. Coys will arrange the Parade hours in the morning NCOs & men attending Classes will be excused the Parade	

Jennings Blake.

RETURN shewing decrease in Strength for the
month of December

	Off	OR
Strength of Unit, 1st December, 1918	45	693

Decrease during month:- Off OR
(a) Demobilized:-
    Coalminers   19
    Pivotals   2
    Long Service   1
    Watford Details   5
    etc. etc.   27   27

(b) Evacuated sick and struck   2   61
    off strength

(c) Other causes

Strength of Unit, 1st January, 1919.   43 605

(signed)
Capt.
D.O.
1st Batt^n The Essex Regt.

75
appendix 4

1ST ESSEX REGT - OPERATION ORDER NO. 76

REF MAP   Copy No. 11
VALENCIENNES
Sheet 12
1/100-000

1. Brigade Field Operations will take place on Thursday 12th inst.

2. The 1st Essex Regt will take part, and is allotted a frontage of approx 3000 yards.

3. Frontages and Assembly positions areas follows:-
   13th R.Fs.   Along the line of the railway from where it crosses the RUISSEAU DE SART at 3.I.55.60 to HALTE (3.I.15.60)
   1st Essex Regt. From HALTE to the L of WARGNIES-LE-GRAND, thence to the W of WARGNIES-LE-GRAND thence to the road junction due EAST of point 370 (3.I.13.80) Brigade H
   Brigade H.Q. and 112th T.M.B. From the road junction at 3.I.14.80 to the road junction 900 yards due East of the Y. in BRY 3.I.22.82.
   1st Herts From the Road junction at 3.I.22.8. along the track passing through the first A in BEAUREGARD to the junction of the RUISSEAU DE SART and the railway.

4. The objective is a point on the high ground at about 3.I.32.70.

5. Formation will be the whole battalion extended in single rank at about ten paces interval.

6. The advance will take place at Zero. Ranks will gradually close in as the advance towards the objective continues.
   After ZERO the advance will be checked, and resumed on the bugle calls "Standfast" and "Carry on"

7. A mounted Officer will guide the centre of the battalion, and there will be a mounted Officer on each flank to keep touch with units right and left. These officers must NOT be in advance of the line.

8. Patches of sown land are not to be crossed but must be encircled.

9. From ZERO to ZERO plus 15 minutes the advance will be at the rate of 100 yards in 3 minutes. The advance will then be halted by Bugle Call, and section leaders will advance from the ranks. Ranks will then close up, and the advance be resumed while section leaders proceed to "Mop up" in the centre.

10. ZERO will be at 0930 hours.

11. The battalion frontage will be divided as follows: "W" Coy on the right, from HALTE to bottom of L in WARGNIES-LE-GRAND. "X" Coy - right centre, from point detailed as left flank of "W" Coy to top of W in WARGNIES-LE-GRAND. "Y" Coy. - left centre, from point detailed as left flank of "X" Coy to point halfway along track leading to left flank of Battalion. "Z" Coy on the left, from point detailed as left flank of "Y" Coy to road junction 3.I.14.80.

12. Companies will report present, and on alignment, by mounted orderly to the Adjutant at junction of tracks immediately N.W. of W in WARGNIES-LE-GRAND by ZERO minus 15 minutes.

13. Dress will be clean fatigue, each man will carry his water proof sheet. Each man will carry an entrenching tool handle. No other arms or equipment will be taken.

14. Each company will have its charger on parade, but only those officers detailed by the Adjutant will ride after ZERO to completion of operation

15. Strict control must be maintained to prevent loss of direction and breaking the ranks.

16. Signalling Officer will arrange to distribute a proportion of Signallers with flags to each company. These men will be distributed through the ranks of the companies.

17. All battalion runners, not on duty, otherwise, will parade under L/c Surrey MM. and will meet the Adjutant at the point where coys. have been ordered to report to him at ZERO minus 15 minutes. ALL other personnel of B.H.Q. on parade will be with their companies.

18. Watches will be synchronised with Signalling Officer at B.H.Q. at 0800 hours 12th instant.

Issued at 1600 hours.

H.S.Daly
Lieutenant
A/Adjutant 1st Battn. the Essex Regiment.

Distribution
No. 1.	-	C.O.	No. 7.	-	B.H.Q. Mess
No. 2.	-	112th Inf bde.	No. 8.	-	R.S.M.
No. 3.	-	"W" Coy	No. 9.	-	T.O.
No. 4.	-	"X" "	No. 10.	-	File
No. 5.	-	"Y" "	No. 11.	-	War Diary
No. 6.	-	"Z" "	No. 12.	-	"

appendix III

1ST. ESSEX OPERATION ORDERS NO. 76.

Map.Ref. 1/100,000
VALENCIENNES. (Sheet 12.)
NAMUR. (Sheet 8).
BRUSSELS (Sheet 6.)

Copy No. 11

13th. Dec/18.

No. 1.   The 37th. Division will march to GOSSELIES Area commencing tomorrow 14th. December.

2.   The Battalion will be formed up on Battn. Parade Ground, ready to move off, at 1145 hrs., march to BELLIGNIES, and will be billetted there for the night.

3.   The Battalion will pass Brigade Starting Point - Road Junction ¼-mile South of S in LA BOIS CRETTE at 1241 hours.

4.   Order of march - Headquarters, "W", "X", "Y", Drums, "Z".

5.   DRESS - Full marching order.   Waterproof-sheets will be rolled, and placed on top of the pack, underneath the flap. Steel helmets on the back of the pack.   Box Respirators will be carried.

6.   Distances between Coys. - 10 yards.
     "   "   "Z" Coy & Transport - 10 yards.

7.   O. C. "Y" Company will detail one Officer and his platoon to march in rear of the Transport, and pick up all stragglers.   The M.O. will be with this party, and will give a chit to any man, who is unable to march, to join the F. A. in rear.

8.   No man is to fall out without a chit from an Officer.

9.   Any man falling out, and told by the M.O. to join the Ambulance, will sit at the side of the Road till the F.A. comes up to him.   He will then hand his chit to an Officer of the F. A.

10.   All watches will be synchronised on parade at 1145.hrs.

11.   Blankets in bundles of 10, and Jerkins in bundles of 5, will be stacked at Q.M. Stores by 0800 hrs.   Officers' kits to be at Q.M. Stores by 0930 hrs.   The Mess Cart will go round Company Messes and collect mess boxes at 1030 hrs. Two mess boxes per Company only allowed.

12.   All surplus kits, and mess boxes not required at BELLIGNIES, will be dumped at Q.M. Stores by 0800 hrs.   These will be taken direct to La LONGUEVILLE.

13.   O.C. Coys. will report to B.H.Q., when their Coys. are billetted.

14.   Acknowledge.

Issued at 1945 hours.

J.A.Mackay Paxton
Captain & Adjutant,
1st. Battn. The Essex Regiment.

Distribution:-
```
No. 1 - C.O.,                   No. 7. - S.O. & I.O.
 "  2 - "W" Coy.                 "  8. - Q.M. & T.O.
 "  3 - "X"  "                   "  9. - R.S.M.
 "  4 - "Y"  "                   " 10. - War Diary.
 "  5 - "Z"  "                   " 11. -   -do-
 "  6 - 112th. Inf. Bgde.        " 12. - File.
```

1st Bn. The Essex Regt. - Operation Order No. 77
Appendix IV   Copy No. 10
14-12-18

Reference Sheet - 1/100,000.
Valenciennes (Sheet 12)
Namur (Sheet 8)
Brussels (Sheet 6)

1. The 37th Division will continue the march to GOSSELIES area tomorrow.
2. The Battalion will march to NEUF MESNIL, and be billetted there.
3. Batt. Starting Point - B.H.Q. Mess.
4. Order of march - H.Qrs., X, Y, Z, Drums, W.
   B.H.Q. will pass Bn. Starting Point at 1420 hrs.
   Distances between companies the same as to-day. Distances between Transport as in Addendum to 112th Inf. Bde. Order No. 252 of 13/12/18.
5. Dress - same as in Operation Order No. 76 of 13/12/18.
6. Blankets rolled in bundles of ten will be at Q.M. Stores by 0830 hrs.
   Officers' Kits by 1000 hrs. The Mess Cart will collect Mess Boxes at 1345 hrs.
7. <u>Saluting</u>. The only procedure when passing a General Officer is that each officer will salute. Transport drivers do not salute.
8. O.C. 'Z' Coy. will detail 1 Officer and his platoon to march in rear of Transport to collect stragglers. Other orders regarding stragglers are the same as in Operation Order No. 76.
9. O.C. Coys, Q.M. and Transport <u>must</u> report when they are in billets as soon as possible.
10. Reveille - 0730 hrs.   H.O.R - 1000 hrs.
    Breakfast - 0830 hrs.   Dinners - 1230 hrs.
    Sick - 0915 hrs.
11. Acknowledge.

Issued at 2000 hrs.

J.M. Mackay Paston
Capt. & Adjt.
1st Bn. The Essex Regiment

Distribution:
No. 1 - C.O.   No. 7 - Q.M. & T.O.
   2 - W. Coy.   8 - I.O., S.O., M.O.
   3 - X "   9 - R.S.M.
   4 - Y "   10 - War Diary
   5 - Z "   11 -
   6 - 112th Inf. Bde.   12 - File.

appendix V

1ST ESSEX REGT - OPERATION ORDER NO.76.

Copy No. 10

REF MAP
1/100,000
VALENCIENNES (Sheet 12)
NAMUR (Sheet 8)
BRUSSELS (Sheet 6)

Dec. 16 1918.

1. The 37th Div. will continue its march tomorrow.

2. The Battalion will march to MAIRIEUX, and be billetted there.

3. Battalion starting point - Battalion Hqr. Mess.

4. Order of March - Headquarters, "Y", "Z", Color party, "W", Drums, "X". Headquarters will pass Battalion starting point at 1010 hrs.

5. Blankets in bundles of 10 to be at Q.M.Stores by 0830 hrs. Officers' Kits by 0900 hrs. Mess Cart will collect Mess boxes (two per coy.) at 0930 hrs.

6. O.C."X" Coy will detail 1 Off. and his platoon to march in rear of the Transport to pick up stragglers.

7. Reveille - 0730 hrs.   Orderly Room 1430 hrs.
   Breakfast 0830 hrs.   Dinners on arrival.
   Sick   0900 hrs.

8. Other orders as in Operation Order 77.

9. Acknowledge.

Issued at 2200 Hrs.

G.A.Mackay Parker
Captain & Adjutant.
1st. Battn. The Essex Regiment.

Distribution

No.	1.	-	O.C.
"	2.	-	"W" Coy
"	3.	-	"X" "
"	4.	-	"Y" "
"	5.	-	"Z" "
"	6.	-	112th Inf. Bde.
"	7.	-	Q.M. & T.O.
"	8.	-	B.H.Q. Offs. Mess
"	9.	-	R.S.M.
"	10.	-	War Diary
"	11.	-	" "
"	12.	-	File

1st Bn. The Essex Regt. Operation Orders 79.

Appendix VI

Ref Map: 1/100,000
Valenciennes (Sheet 12)
Namur (Sheet 8)

Copy No. 11

17-12-18.

1. The 37th Division will continue its march to GOSSELIES tomorrow.
2. The Bn. will march to BINCHE tomorrow, and will be billeted there.
3. Bn. Starting Point will be the CHURCH, HAIRIEUX.
4. Order of March – H.Q., Z, W, Colour Party, X, Drums, Y.
   B.H.Q. will pass Bn. Starting Point at 0930 hrs.
5. Blankets and Officers' Kits of W and X Coys will be dumped outside their Coy. H.Q. by 0730 hrs, when they will be collected by lorry. The lorry will then proceed to Z Coy. Blankets & Kits of this Coy should be dumped outside the Coy. H.Q. by 0800 hrs. Blankets & Officers' Kits of Y Coy & B H.Q. to be at Q.M.S Stores by 0830 hrs. The mess cart will go round and collect mess gear starting with W and X Coys at 0830 hrs.
6. O.C. 'Y' Coy. will detail 1 officer and his platoon to march in rear of transport to pick up stragglers.
7. Reveille – 0630 hrs.   Dinners – on Halt.
   Breakfast – 0730 hrs.   Orderly Room – hour will be notified later.
   S.v.k. – 0815 hrs.
8. Other orders as in Operation Orders No. 76, 77 & 78.
9. Acknowledge.

Issued at 1800 hrs.

J.A. Mackay Park
Capt & A/jt
1st Bn. The Essex Regiment

Distribution
No. 1 – C.O.
    2 – 'W' Coy
    3 – X
    4 – Y
    5 – Z
    6 – 112th Inf Bde

No. 7 – Q.M. & T.O.
    8 – B. H.Q. Mess
    9 – R.S.M.
    10 – War Diary
    11 –
    12 – File.

1st Bn The Essex Regt. Operation Order. 80

Ref Sheet 1/100,000　　　Appendix VII　　　Copy No 10
Namur (Sheet 8)　　　　　　　　　　　　　　18/12/18
Brussels (Sheet 6)

1. The march to GOSSELIES will be continued tomorrow.
2. The Bn will march to FORCHIES area, and be billetted there.
3. Bn. starting point - The Square, BINCHE.
4. Order of march - B.H.Q, Drums, "W" "X" Color Party, "Y" "Z". BHQ will enter the square at 0955 hrs.
5. Blankets rolled in bundles of ten will be taken to Q.M Stores by 0800 hrs. Officers kits by 0830 hrs. Mess cart will collect Mess Boxes (2 per Coy) at 0845 hrs, commencing with "Z" Coy.
6. Reveille - 0700 hrs　　Dinners on arrival
   Breakfast - 0800　"　　Hour for Bn O.R will be on
   Sick - 0845　"　　arrival, exact hour to be notified later.
7. O.C "Z" Coy will detail 1 Officer and his platoon to follow in rear of Transport to pick up stragglers.
8. Other orders as in previous operation orders.
9. Acknowledge.

Issued at 1830 hrs

　　　　　　　　　　　　　　G.A. Mackay Prior
　　　　　　　　　　　　　　Capt + Adjt
　　　　　　　　　　　　　　1st Bn The Essex Regt.

Distribution
No 1 - C.O　　　　　No 7 - Q.M + T.O
" 2 - "W" Coy　　　" 8 - Bn H.Q mess
" 3 - "X" "　　　　" 9 - R S M
" 4 - "Y" "　　　　" 10 - War Diary
" 5 - "Z" "　　　　" 11 - "　"
" 6 - 112th Bde　　　" 12 - File

Appendix VIII

Copy No 12

17/10/18

Maps 1/100,000
Namur (Sheet 5)
Brussels (Sheet 6)

1. The 3rd Division will continue its march to GOSSELIES area.

2. The Battalion will march to RANSART and be billeted there.

3. Battalion starting point - B.H.Q. Officers Mess

4. Order of March - B.H.Q., X, Y, Coluur thirty Z, W (known)

5. B.H.Q. will pass starting point at 0910 hours. Blankets in bundles of ten to be in Q.M. Stores by 0730 hours. Officers kits by 0730 hours. Mess Cart will collect Mess boxes (6 per coy) at 0800 hours.

6. O.C. "W" Coy will detail one Officer and his platoon to march in rear of transport to collect stragglers.

7. Reveille   0630 hrs.   Orderly Room on arrival
   Breakfast 0730 "   hours to be notified later.
   Sick   0815 "   Rummers on arrival.

8. Other orders as in previous Operation Orders

9. Acknowledge.

Issued at 2130 hrs.

G.A. Mackay Paxton Capt
Adjt 1st/5th The Essex Regt

Distribution

No 1 - C.O.   No 7 - Q.M. & T.O.
   2 - "W"   8 - Bn H.Q. Mess
   3 - X   9 - R.S.M.
   4 - Y   10 - War Diary
   5 - Z   11 - "   "
   6 - M.G. Pltn   12 - File

1st Bn. The Essex Regt.

War Diary.

Volume XLVII

January 1919.

WAR DIARY

INTELLIGENCE SUMMARY.

(Erase heading not required.)

Army Form C. 2118.

Place	Date	Hour	Summary of Events and Information	Remarks and references to Appendices
RANSART	JAN 1919 1		7 hrs Parade under Company arrangements. Educational Classes — Army Certificates — French — English	WSM
"	2	1000	Lecture in Battalion Concert Hall all Coys & BHQ Ranks on "History as a Study." Educational Classes — Army Certificates — English — French	WSM
"	3		7 hrs Parade under Company arrangements. Educational Classes — Army Certificates — English — French	WSM
"	4		Educational Classes	WSM
"	5	0930	Battalion Church Parade	WSM
"	6		7 hrs Parade under Company arrangement	WSM
"	7		Educational Classes	WSM
"	8		7 hrs Parade under Company arrangement	WSM
"	9		Educational Classes	WSM
"	10		Army Certificates — English — Shorthand — French	WSM

Army Form C. 2118.

WAR DIARY

INTELLIGENCE SUMMARY

(Erase heading not required.)

Instructions regarding War Diaries and Intelligence Summaries are contained in F. S. Regs., Part II. and the Staff Manual respectively. Title pages will be prepared in manuscript.

Place	Date	Hour	Summary of Events and Information	Remarks and references to Appendices
	JAN 1919			
RANSART	11		1hrs parade under Company arrangements	wmm
"	12	10.15	BATTALION CHURCH PARADE	wmm
"	13		1hrs PARADE under Company Arrangements, Educational Classes wmm	
"	14		" "	wmm
"	15	14.00	LECTURE AT BDE CINEMA SUBJECT BATTLE OF ZEEBRUGGE by MAJOR SMITH 112 INF BDE	wmm
"	16	09.30	The Battn was inspected by Bde General commanding 112th INF BDE	wmm
"	17		1hrs Parade under Company arrangements	wmm
"	18		Inspection of Billets + Educational Classes	wmm
"	19		Battalion Church Parade	wmm
"	20		1hrs Parade under Company Arrangements.	wmm

WAR DIARY

Army Form C. 2118.

(Erase heading not required.)

Instructions regarding War Diaries and Intelligence Summaries are contained in F. S. Regs., Part II. and the Staff Manual respectively. Title pages will be prepared in manuscript.

Place	Date JAN	Hour	Summary of Events and Information	Remarks and references to Appendices
RANSART	21		1 hr. Parade under Company Arrangements.	W.704.
"	22.		The Battalion Bathed - Educational Classes	W.704.
"	23.	0930	Inspection of Box Respirators - Lecture by the Divisional Education Officer. Subject "The Battle of Waterloo"	W.704.
"	24.		Parades under Company Arrangements.	W.704.
"	25.		Inspection by Brigadier	W.704.
"	26.		BATTALION CHURCH PARADE	W.704.
"	27.		The Battalion Bathed	W.704.
"	28.	1100	Lecture in the Cinema. Subject "Empire & Reconstruction" Inter Company Competition for the CO's Cup BEST TURNED OUT COY "W" Company - BEST COY Marching Past "Z" Coy "W" Coy in Reserve awarded 150 points - "Z" Coy 50 points	W.704. W.704.
"	29.		ARMY CERTIFICATE CLASSES	W.704.
"	30		ARMY CERTIFICATE CLASSES	W.704.
"	31		"	W.704.

The Bottom Bathed

Vernon F. Blake.

RETURN SHEWING DECREASE IN STRENGTH FOR THE MONTH OF - JAN.

STRENGTH OF UNIT JAN 1ST 1919 - 44 OFFS - 681 ORs.

	OFF	O.R.
	44	681

DECREASE DURING MONTH:-

	OFF	OR
(a) DEMOBILIZED	7	131
COAL MINERS		1
PIVOTALS		7
LONG SERVICE		18
WATFORD DETAILS		18
etc. etc.		4
	7	179

	OFF	OR
	7	179
(b) EVACUATED SICK + STRUCK OFF STRENGTH	1	9
	1	9

(c) OTHER CAUSES

STRENGTH OF UNIT FEB 1ST 1919 36 - 493

	36	493

CONFIDENTIAL

WAR DIARY

OF

1ST BN THE ESSEX REGT.

FOR THE MONTH OF

FEBRUARY 1919.

VOLUME 48.

WAR DIARY

Army Form C. 2118.

(Erase heading not required.)

Instructions regarding War Diaries and Intelligence Summaries are contained in F. S. Regs., Part II. and the Staff Manual respectively. Title pages will be prepared in manuscript.

Place	Date	Hour	Summary of Events and Information	Remarks and references to Appendices
AHNSART	FEB 1		Kit Inspection & Educational classes	
"	2		Battalion Church Parade	
"	3		Parades under Company arrangements	
"	4		Coy parade under Company arrangement	
"	5		Coy parade under Company arrangement. Bugle Bd Bright	
"	6		Brigade Group Deployment at Brigade	
"	7		Men Parade during day to bathing. Whole of Batt. being examined Throne Light M.G - Lewis gunners & Signallers to Battn	
"	8		Battn Parade. Lecture given for Lecture by lt. – Infant Pres 60 Month on The British Soldier. Kit & Billet inspection under Company arrangements Resp.	
"	9		Battn Church Parade	
"	10		The Batt. Gutted	
"	11		All available men for fatigue	
"	12		2 Officers + 60 OR. were transferred to the 25th Battn (Army of Occupation)	

Army Form C. 2118.

WAR DIARY
of
INTELLIGENCE SUMMARY.

(Erase heading not required.)

Instructions regarding War Diaries and Intelligence Summaries are contained in F. S. Regs., Part II. and the Staff Manual respectively. Title pages will be prepared in manuscript.

Place	Date FEB	Hour	Summary of Events and Information	Remarks and references to Appendices
RAMSAFF	13		All completed men were engaged on Regimental Duties	
	14		"	
	15		Returns church parade	
	16		"	
	17		Parades paraded for to start of Battl Reg'l at HQHQ	
	18		C.O. read out the Army & Navy of [illegible] on [illegible] Rifle M.G.	
	19			
	20		The Battl Carried out [illegible] hour on 14 Lewis Gun [illegible] Bayn Drill	
	21		Companies [illegible] on the work that the companies [illegible] also were engaged on Trench & Wire School	
	22			
	23		Parade Church Parade	
	24		All available men were engaged on Trenches & Wire School	

WAR DIARY

(Erase heading not required.)

Place	Date	Hour	Summary of Events and Information	Remarks and references to Appendices
TRANSAGT	FEB 25		The Battalion detail all completed. No one being engaged on Reported Guards duty.	
"	26			
"	27			
"	28		Nominal Roll meeting	

RETURN SHEWING DECREASE IN STRENGTH FOR THE MONTH OF - FEB.

STRENGTH OF UNIT 1st FEB 1919 35 - 556

	OFF	O.R
	35	556

DECREASE DURING MONTH :- OFF   O.R

(a) DEMOBILIZED
  COAL MINERS
  PIVOTALS   3
  LONG SERVICE   24
  ~~~~~~~~~~~ P.G.   2   162
                         2   189

	OFF	OR
	2	189

(b) EVACUATED SICK + STRUCK OFF
    STRENGTH   3   3

(c) OTHER CAUSES   6   73   6   73
                                   (2)   (60)   (2)   (60)

STRENGTH OF UNIT 1st MARCH 1919 27 - 291

	27	291

H. Daly Lt.
1st Bn THE ESSEX Regt.

28.2.19.

Reprinted from The "Southend Standard, March 2nd, 1922.

OUT OF THE IRISH FREE STATE.

1st Battalion, Essex Regiment, moves from Kinsale to Carrickfergus.

DIFFICULTIES, DANGERS AND DESPERADOES.   **SCENES AND INCIDENTS.**

(By "*Spectator*.")

FOREWORD.

"Irish Mail via Fishguard." The notice caught my eye at Paddington and pleased me. I had come post-haste from Sussex overnight; there, in a pleasant hotel at Bexhill, facing a tumultuous sea, I had done nothing for four days, with marked advantage to an enfeebled frame; I was the better for my idling. But, as Keats superfluously says, there comes an end to everything; the telephone put a period to my loafing; evening saw me again in London; night in Southend; next morning, nothing loth, I got marching orders for Kinsale. That—just that—is my idea of a stirring, profitable life; I love to visit places and to write about them afterwards. And so, when I saw the Irish Mail at Paddington, I delighted therein. Never before had I been to Ireland, that country of a hundred charms and a thousand sorrows. Here was the promise of yet another experience; here was one more turn in the kaleidoscope of life. To be sure, my journey was destined to be fraught with some danger, but of that I had no prevision. In the early days of the Great War, I went from Copenhagen to Liverpool, and from Tilbury to Rotterdam and back, when every sea swarmed with mines; such things are what Sam Weller might call the "trimmings" of my profession. Nor could I foresee how unkind the elements would prove. It rained or snowed all the time I was in Ireland; I do not suppose it has ceased, as I write, to do the one or the other.

WHY I WENT.

Macaulay, eighty-three years ago, sat down to begin his History of England. In his second paragraph he referred to Ireland as cursed by the domination of race over race, of religion over religion; it was, he wrote, still a member of the Empire, but "a withered and distorted member." He added that Ireland contributed no strength to the body politic, but was reproachfully pointed at by all who feared or envied the greatness of England. To-day he might have written identical words as truly. In consequence, English troops are to-day, as so often before, in Ireland, endeavouring to contribute to its peaceful settlement. Among them is the 1st Battalion, Essex Regiment, busied, as formerly in many lands, with an infinity of useful service. That body I was to join for a few hours at Kinsale, prior to their departure for Carrickfergus, Ulster, whereby the Irish Free State was evacuated by them. I was sure of a warm welcome. On several fronts, throughout the late war, the *Southend Standard* reached each battalion of the regiment on service overseas; it was read at all hours, pored over in a hundred trenches, discussed in numberless dug-outs. Photographs therefrom adorned the walls of huts, from Ypres to Peronne, from Boulogne to Cambrai; acknowledgments of its receipt, on field cards or by letter, reached Southend daily, month after month, through all those terrible times. For that reason and because I had previous experience of the hospitality of the regiment, I was sure, I repeat, of a hearty welcome at Kinsale. I was not disappointed.

Further, I went to Kinsale for details of battalion activities in the south of Ireland. I may mention, here and now, that the higher civilian classes in that land are greatly annoyed—many are exasperated—by the meagre reports of Irish news. They regard the London newspapers as hopelessly misleading, so little do they convey to Englishmen of the true state of that "most distressful country," Ireland. Violent outrages have been committed hourly; few are so much as mentioned by the Press, and it is felt that we, in England, have in consequence no true conception of the anxieties and horrors shared by our countrymen, as by others, throughout many areas. Above all, fear is felt of what may happen in any district from which the military are withdrawn. Thefts, burning, maltreatments of many kinds took place under the eyes of our soldiers; if these things were done in the green tree, what might be done in the dry? In a word, it is felt that the helpless position of the "Irish loyalist," in particular, is not realized; otherwise, say some, much sterner and stronger measures would surely have been taken to preserve the peace. Thus it chanced that I set out for Ireland at a time when grievances waited for visiting ears; I was to hear far more than I could note or remember. Moreover, note-taking in Ireland has its perils —but more of this presently.

ON THE WAY.

I left Paddington in darkness and was sorry. For I love the rolling panorama of travel, especially as seen from the windows of a swift train; as Stevenson says, there are worse ways of seeing the country than from a railway carriage. In the circumstances I tried to doze; but I had plenty to think about and sleep fled from me. A negro, bound for a ship at Cardiff, sat beside me—a most friendly fellow, who, on encouragement from my side, would doubtless have told me all his joys and sorrows. But for once I was the dull dog; I kept my counsel; he subsided into slumber. The train thundered on through the night, and by way of Reading, Swindon, Landore, Carmarthen, drew me to Fishguard. Often as I have been as far as Carmarthen, I had never before got to this newly risen port; again I deplored the darkness. For the rise of Fishguard is a story typical of English and Welsh enterprise; it is one of the romances of commerce and of travel; gladly would I have looked about me in broad daylight, to see what manner of place it was. Only since 1906 has the Fishguard route to Ireland been in use; Satan himself could with difficulty have augmented the impediments of site and circumstance. Indeed, the site itself was created by blasting the surrounding hills; a quay wall was constructed in the bay and the intervening space filled in; six miles of lines and sidings were laid down, on ground cleared by the blasting of two million tons of rock, to accomplish which, engineers, at the first, carted their tools to the top of Pen Gw, three hundred feet above the adjacent sea. As it was, I saw nothing of Fishguard, saving the light on the near breakwater, and the brightly lit platform against which the steamer lay. We had an easy passage to Rosslare. Here my curiosity was no better rewarded. It was still dark when the boat drew alongside; I had been warned that my bag might be examined, but this was not done. Indeed, so insignificant did I appear that no man interrogated me, and in two minutes I was seated in an Irish train. Grey dawn was all about me as Waterford was reached; I noticed the fern-freckled cliff that overshadows the station on the northern side; a jackdaw, walking most comically, now on a sleeper and now on a metal, eyed me very suspiciously as I watched his progress. We drew away, continuing the long, Sunday morning journey of six hours towards Cork. We stopped at every station; small boys, raucous and insistent, sold the Dublin *Saturday Herald*. I fell upon it with avidity. I learned, with little surprise, that matters were not quiet in Belfast; that De Valera had cabled to Massachusetts, to "The National Treasurer of the Association for the Recognition of the Irish Republic," thanking him for receipt of funds and urging members not to forget that "the Republic still exists." It interested me more to learn that De Valera (that very active man) had but just passed down from Dublin, and was then in Cork, where a great demonstration was to take place that day

TYPICAL OF THE TERROR.

I turned the page. Here, under my eyes, was a story to the point, and it came from Waterford. It seemed that on Friday evening, one Kitty Paul, a girl of 14 years, was taken from her home by four masked men. They drove her, in a motor car, to the old munition factory at Bilberry, about one mile distant. She was questioned touching her brother, a prominent Waterford Volunteer. She replied she could tell them nothing and one man threatened to shoot her. "Shoot away," said the girl. Thereupon the contents of a bottle were forced down her throat. She became unconscious, and was left alone. Later, coming to herself, she stumbled weakly from the factory, was recognized by friends near the quay, and was taken home in a dazed condition. Her mother, earlier in the day, found a notice thrust under the door: "Daughter Kitty's life is in danger. Beware!" Subsequently, she noticed writing on the kitchen table: "We are taking your daughter Kitty away. If the information we want is not forthcoming, it means death to her." The report added that a fortnight previously the girl was found gagged in the house, early in the morning; two of the men who kidnapped her were, she asserted, concerned in the gagging; further, it was stated that the I.R.A. were "investigating the matter."

This incident was one among many. In Limerick, the same evening, Loughlin McDwards, a policeman and a native of Edinburgh, was shot dead by an unknown party; next morning, the Ex-Service Legion Club, Sligo, was burned to the ground. The only occupant, who lost a leg in the Great War, with difficulty got away; cause unknown or persons not known. I bought other papers as we drew in, and all had such stories to tell.

TOWARDS CORK.

I was not particularly impressed by the scenery. For the most part, rolling country stretches from Rosslare to Cork, with few outstanding features. Around Kilmacthomas gorse and fir and pine are sprinkled profusely over a land of rippling streams; there as elsewhere the bare rock crops out from lush greensward or heathery hill; now and then a jaunting car crosses a valley or moves across the skyline; now and then a ruined tower or deserted, tumbling cottage catches the eye. Dungarven shows finer prospects; here the Colligan river bisects the town; the sea washes almost to the railway, reminding me of Carmarthen Bay; I was sorry that the islets in the Bay, and the headland beyond, were partly hidden in mist. We came to Lismore, so long the residence of bishops; the manor was held by Sir Walter Raleigh; the parish formerly bore that almost impronounceable name, Magsbciath. By this it was broad morning; at each station a few natives gathered to meet the mail; plenty of most lively Gaelic was heard. But they boarded the train; the day before, one heard, all trains were filled with patriots eager to reach Cork in time for the demonstration. We were nearing Blarney when a jolly Irishman joined us, concertina in hand; in the corridor, passing from carriage to carriage, he played lively jigs, and collected coppers in a tin. At Blarney a couple of Irish lasses, obviously good-humoured, came into my compartment, bribing the musician to prolong the strains. I had passed along the train meantime, noting a few sinister faces and hearing a deal of chatter. One topic, I fancied, was of outstanding importance. The Black and Tans—thank heaven!—were now a name only. For this might God be praised, for God, as Father O'Murphy tells, is always good.

A CITY OF CONFUSION.

At Cork, it would seem, human affairs are always at floodtide; they have been so, I fancy, since, in the year 821, men from some fleet burned the "city"—you may read all about it in the "Annals of the Four Masters." Of these and other matters I heard, years back, from the Vicar of St. Erkenwald's, Southend—a native of Cork and a Freeman of that city; also, from friend Thackeray, of Hitchin, who may see this article and will rejoice accordingly. There was a deal of bustle, certainly, as I left the station, and rode, in a little 'bus, to the Imperial Hotel. There, as I stood in the entrance hall, a tall, saturnine man spoke confidentially with one of the staff. It was De Valera, who, I will add at once, slept in Cork that night with a strong, fully armed guard posted outside his room. The head waiter, of harassed mien, brought me my meal with his own hands; he was, I thought, glad to serve and be done with me, for the lunch hour was not yet, and he was burdened with preparations for the President and other guests.

It seemed a drab, wet, unpleasant city as I walked presently in the lower quarters. Were Cork colonnaded I should think it like Bologna. Bare-footed urchins ran from side to side, selling newspapers and themselves gathering news. For—as the reader will soon hear if in Cork—these gamins fetch and carry information of most secret character; you pause to make an inquiry, and forthwith, as though by magic, one comes alongside to learn your business. You may by no means evade their effrontery; "They man the chariot and they board the barge." First and foremost, are you a stranger? The farther you have come the more closely you will be watched and listened to, and the more likely your goings are to be reported. They peer and poke and pry with almost preternatural cunning; Sinn Fein leaders soon know where you are staying, for the secret intelligence boys, as you emerge from the station, or get from your car, follow to your hotel or lodgings. You can hardly play dumb dog all day; you have but to ask for such and such streets, or to say "Thank you" as you buy the *Cork Examiner* or *Irish Times* and you are known for an Englishman—for the Republican's most hated foe. If conscious that you are followed by one of these sleuthhounds, buy *The Freeman's Journal*. It is good advice.

I did not go to the great demonstration. I was strongly urged to absent myself therefrom; the feeling prevalent in Cork was explained; perhaps I should, rather, say the "feelings," for opinions are something more than mixed in that city of confusion. De Valera—the Irish newspapers told me—had a strong following in the city; but so, I learned, had Mr. Collins, and his turn was coming next; he, too, was to address a great meeting soon. But I gathered something of what took place; how De Valera, as chief speaker, read resolutions and spoke thereto; how, as he sat on No. 1 platform, before business began, an old woman mounted to where he was, opened fire upon him with fine powers of invective, and caused no small sensation. Rumour ran that she said: "What the divil is your business here, anyway? It's the Free State we've got, and mean to keep, so you may just hop back to your own place, and leave us to mind our own affairs." The sentiments expressed, at least, are probably near the mark, and were evidently shared by many around her, for she took her own time to dismount, and walked away unmolested. The gathering was no doubt large, as it appeared in a photograph in the *Cork Examiner*, but there was, apparently, considerable apathy displayed. Hundreds, I was told, joined the fringe of the crowd, listened for a few minutes to De Valera, the Lord Mayor of Cork, Miss MacSwiney, Countess Markiewicz or other speakers and turned away. No uproar followed.

A MEMORABLE RIDE.

I had two disappointments in Cork, and was brought to the verge of desperation. On Sunday, on arriving, I learned that no train ran that day to Kinsale. Nor could I hear of any other conveyance going that way: so I stayed in the city, twiddling my thumbs in sheer impotence, hearing things useful, seeing sights memorable, and waiting for the morning. But worse followed. There was a train, I was told, at 9 o'clock next morning; but surely I, a journalist from England, had no thought of travelling by it! Why, it would be full of men and women of Sinn Fein views and practices, returning west after their joy-ride to hear De Valera; Press men had on several occasions been threatened; one, but the other day, arrested; it would be asking for trouble to ride in such company. Here was a pretty pass. I went to the military barracks on the hill top, early on Monday morning. No transport was going to Kinsale; in the town, possibly, I might get some tradesman to give me a lift if he were were driving that way—a very improbable slice of luck.

And so, in a quandary, I talked over the telephone with somebody at Kinsale—one of the Regiment, whose voice reached me so faintly as to be hardly audible. His advice jumped with that already given; for speed was imperative—the battalion was leaving that night. I returned to the lower town, and there talked business with young Mr. Celty, to whom I was strongly recommended to explain the situation. He rose to the occasion, and I could have fallen on his neck. In a few minutes he would have an excellent car ready; in an hour I should reach Kinsale; he would have me set down at the entrance to the barracks. I can see him as I write, as he stood near the entrance to his garage; I shall remember him to the end as a rescuer in the hour of need. Did he think the journey quite safe? Well, there was his car, worth £800 to him; he would hardly risk its destruction, or even its damage, were he not confident I should not be stopped. This ran with what I had been told; my helper was a man widely known and respected; he drove "ordinary people, commercials and the like," all over the district, and stood in little fear of trouble. So I made my bargain, giving Treasury notes in exchange for a receipt bearing the stamp of the Irish Free State, and his promise proved good.

The car was driven by a man good and true, who knew the country as I long knew the face of my father. The main roads were still defaced and endangered by trenches; bridges, long since blown up, were but partly restored—propped up by timbers and perilous save for light vehicles; red flags hung above them to warn drivers of the fact. In consequence, the route was marked by the strangest divagations; for twenty odd miles I saw no village, nor was there much sign of life; the narrow roads, sometimes little more than lanes, were in places so flooded that water flew far and wide as we rushed past. The weather was of the ficklest; at times rain fell in torrents, driven across the car by fitful gusts; at times the clouds parted, and bright sunshine streamed through a little stretch of blue. The country grew more wooded as we neared Kinsale, and was well diversified. The water on my right, said the chauffeur, was "just the sea"; it ran far inland thereabouts; in point of fact, it was the Bandon River.

"AT LAST!"

It was just one o'clock when, turning suddenly, we mounted to the Military Barracks, on high ground overlooking the harbour of Kinsale. The gate opened to my knock, and my first impression was of a large revolver in a soldier's hand. I told my business, to the accompanying tread of the sentry, pacing a bridge of planks above my head. The O.C.—Lieut.-Col. F. W. Moffitt, D.S.O.—was at luncheon in F. Block, and to him I went I was received most kindly, and enjoyed his hospitality for the rest of the day. It was, as I have said, the battalion's last day at Kinsale; almost everything was already packed for the evacuation; the men, in one respect only, were like Gilpin and his wife, "all agog to dash through thick and thin." All was stir and activity; orderlies and sergeants went to and fro across the great square of the barracks; a troop train, the first of three, was to leave at 2.30 p.m. I went with this party to the station, to watch the entrainment. Rifles were stacked on the platform, amongst a litter of kit and baggage; a few Kinsale girls were allowed to look on, and, incidentally, to bid farewell to the boys. Perhaps, however, it was *au revoir*; a Kinsale jeweller, if rumour ran truly, had of late sold more engagement rings than ever before in all his days! The detachment numbered 39, and was under Lieut. H. Alp, of Shoeburyness, whose father, I learned, founded Alp's Mission, in that far-off, but familiar outpost in England. With him I enjoyed a chat, chiefly concerned with the doings of the battalion; but "the time was not long," as Dr. Johnson said of an equally memorable occasion, and all too soon the train drew away, the boys singing as they went. They were to go straight through to Carrickfergus, and I wondered what the future had in store.

INTERLUDE

That afternoon, during a short spell of what Cowper calls "clear shining after rain"—it was very short indeed—Colonel Moffitt led me to a high part of the barracks, showed me the prospect beneath, and mentioned things of interest in its history. The barracks stand in the parish of Rincurran; the ancient church was recently served, during a holiday, by Rev. J. W. Lindsay, D.D., of Southend. Kinsale, destined to be so closely associated with the history of the Essex Regiment, was founded by the Danes; Lord Orrery, writing to Ormond, once fancifully described the harbour as "one of the noblest in Europe." Perhaps the best view over the place is from near the church; town, harbour and river lie outstretched below; beyond rise the Old Head of Kinsale, the lofty lighthouse; the wide waters of the Atlantic, during calm and sunny hours, clearly reflect the clouds that drift above. To the south-east, three in number, lie the Sovereign Islands, at the entrance to Oyster Haven; to the west, the Seven Heads look down upon Courtmacksherry Bay; westward again the peak of 'The Galley," with its light, is the ultimate sentinel of the district. The history of the town and harbour is of great interest, but I am hardly concerned with it here. I may, however, mention that it embraces stirring records of Spanish invasion and ejection; of the great Marlborough; of James II., who landed at Kinsale in 1690, on his way to fight William III. (his son-in-law) on the Boyne.

BATTALION MATTERS.

The headquarters of the 1st Battalion, Essex Regiment, with its band and drums, arrived at Kinsale on August 31st, 1919. Forthwith it took over the personnel and equipment of the 3rd Battalion (Special Reserve), which went to bed as the 3rd and woke up as the 1st—the old 44th resuscitated yet again. Colonel C. G. Lewis, C.M.G., D.S.O., was then in command, but he relinquished the post on September 26th, and Lieut.-Col. Moffitt was subsequently appointed to succeed him. Many and strange as had been the services of this historic battalion, it was destined, from that time to February 20th, 1922—to go no farther—to add to its history a most remarkable chapter, composed of incidents that transpired in circumstances almost unique even in Irish affairs, which cannot yet be fully narrated.

Difficulties, besetting officers and men alike, were from the first of extraordinary character. A large number of temporary officers, and some 400 of other ranks, were at that time awaiting demobilization; 300 recruits needed prompt and efficient training; N.C.O.'s from other units kept drifting in, to be put into the appointments to which their respective ranks entitled them—whether, in point of fact, they were fitted for these or not, so pressing was the urgency of the moment. In many cases these young N.C.O.'s knew nothing about administrative work in peace conditions; yet these, like even the youngest among the recruits, were destined, to a man, to prove "just about the best fellows in the world"—fellows for whom the "rebels," as the Sinn Feiners are perforce and unfortunately called, soon feared as they feared no other men on this troubled earth. To add to these difficulties, the battalion was divided into halves, one being at Kinsale and Charles Fort (adjacent thereto), (the other at Queenstown) with a small detachment at Bandon drawn from the Ray battalion at Kinsale; the latter half was further subdivided into yet other detachments. At this time, largely by reason of the recruits and demobilization men, the situation was so extremely difficult that Colonel Moffitt and his staff had to "think in individual men"; further, a number of regular officers decided to avail themselves of the liberal gratuity then granted to officers resigning their commissions. In a word, those on whom lay most responsibility slept in no bed of roses.

WHERE WAS "PLEBISCITE"?

Time passed. Many tangled matters were apparently unravelled. Nettles of difficulty were firmly grasped. Then, suddenly, an order was received; the battalion was to move to the "Plebiscite area" of East Prussia. Forthwith all was packed up; everything and everybody was held in readiness, and the two companies at Queenstown were relieved. But the order was as suddenly cancelled. The situation had yielded its modicum of humour. The men, as the story runs, were much puzzled on hearing they were to move to "Plebiscite"; where the (anything you please) was this place, anyway? A N.C.O. stoutly maintained that "Plebiscite" was in the Balkan Peninsula; he knew, because he had been there. But it was destined to remain unknown, and matters closer at hand again made work. Shortly afterwards detachments were formed at Dunmanway, Clonakilty, Timoleague; later, at Bantry and Furious Pier, opposite Bere Island. These measures were due to the campaign of murder started against the R.I.C., and led to enormous difficulties in connection with communications, rations, mails, etc. These difficulties were soon increased by the temporary refusal of the railwaymen to drive soldiers. In consequence, troops and their multiplex baggage—by the Romans so aptly described as *impedimenta*—were for some time everywhere conveyed by lorries. But where will is there a way is found. This action by the railwaymen was finally overcome by a clever method of holding up the trains; soldiers were marched to the stations, put into trains and there kept. The trains in consequence could not run; the civilians in each district grumbled; the railwaymen at length gave way and troops were again conveyed by train. Even then it was hard to find sufficient escorts; but this, too, was a problem solved. In most cases, no doubt, the action of the railwaymen was prompted by fear of consequences; but it was not unassociated with that widespread racial antagonism which, in Cork and many another town in South Ireland, leads the servant to refuse to clean an Englishman's boots.

GUERILLA WARFARE.

About this time a train, escorted by men of another regiment, was fired at by rebels when between Upton and Bandon stations. Five civilians were hit, and in the ensuing action several rebels were killed. Thereafter the latter decided, apparently, that it was unwise to attack trains carrying both civilians and troops, for outrages of this kind ceased. A little later, the detachment at Bantry, and Furious Pier, were relieved; those at Bandon, Dunmanway and Clonakilty were increased. One day, a lorry proceeding to Dunmanway, under Major R. N. Thompson, with eight men, spotted 20 rebels lying in ambush. These the Major attacked, with four men. The rebels promptly fled, throwing away their firearms as they ran; one was captured in a ditch. He was, however, acquitted at his subsequent trial because he was taken without arms. In October, 1920, the situation became yet more serious. By this time fresh lorries had been placed at the disposal of the battalion, and were destined for much rough service. One night, when leaving Newchestown, Major Percival, with two officers and 12 men, was ambushed. Although, as the rebels subsequently admitted, they numbered 40 on that occasion, and fired at the troops when the latter were in lorries and in darkness, the Essex men put up a most gallant fight, losing two officers; three men were wounded. They finally drove back their assailants, bringing in their dead and wounded comrades without the loss of a rifle. For this action Major Percival received the O.B.E.; C.S.M. Benton and Private Woottan the M.B.E. Further, the battalion was congratulated by the Divisional Commander (General Strickland) and the Brigade Commander (General Higginson).

It was, perhaps, a month later when two of our lorries were attacked at Annabeg when proceeding to Cork. A mine was sprung under the second lorry, which was put out of action; Lieut. Dixon (Suffolk Regiment, attached) and two men were killed, and four wounded. Corporal Woodford was among the latter. In the ensuing scrimmage and confusion he was left behind when the first lorry got away, but was later picked up and brought into Cork. He had behaved most courageously and finally, when wounded, had thrown the bolt of his rifle over the hedge to prevent the rebels getting it. At this time constant raids were being made day and night on houses by parties of troops; sometimes a party travelled by lorry, at other times on foot. During these searches a considerable number of rebels were captured; useful information was gained, both from these and captured documents. In one such raid, two "peaceful gentlemen" were taken; they came up to a house after the Essex men had entered it, and were seen by a Corporal to hide something in a wall. Being detained, they proved to be "Brigade Commander Tom Hales" and "Adjutant Hart." In the garden a tin was noticed hanging against a wall; it was kicked away, and behind it was found a magazine containing gun cotton, fuses, etc.

Meantime, the question of information became and remained one of extreme difficulty. Very little could be elicited from the inhabitants; this, and scanty details pieced together from captured documents, had to suffice. Gradually, by these means, a fair knowledge of the area was obtained. Arrested men frequently gave false names, but subsequently, when cross-examined, gave themselves away. For instance, two men were taken; one said he was the other's brother; the other declared he had never seen him before. One man, taken to the house where he said he lived, was confronted with his supposed father, who called him by another name! By such experiences, at length, the troops became very expert in picking out "Shinnies" from other people.

"ACTIVE SERVICE COMPANIES."

It was the beginning of 1921. Matters had gone from bad to worse; the whole area, it seemed, seethed with unrest. By this the rebels had started Active Service Companies, and very active they proved. They consisted of men rightly described by one word only—they were desperadoes. Moving about the country, they billeted themselves on the people. They compelled the local residents to act as outposts, using them as guards at night. These utilized "locals" were often mere ignorant boys, who frequently fell victims to the troops, whilst the more desperate active service men escaped. By this time, too, most of the bridges, far and wide, had been blown up or otherwise destroyed, but there remained, usually, a possible, roundabout route for light horse-vehicles. Flying columns were formed, and these, as will be supposed, kept the rebels on the run. Meantime, the 1st found a draft of 200 men for the 2nd Battalion, and were proportionately depleted. The Band and drums, therefore, were called upon to provide a platoon to augment the strength.

In March information led the battalion to suppose that the enemy's Active Service Companies were in billets north of Crossbarry. The Essex, co-operating with the Hants. Regiment, enveloped the locality. Major Halahan, on entering a house, was fired at by a man coming down the stairs, revolver in hand; he was struck in the chest, but, for some unknown reason, the bullet did not penetrate. Turning quickly, the man tried to escape by the back entrance, but was killed by a sergeant of the regiment; it was subsequently ascertained that he was a Commander. Day was just breaking as heavy firing was heard from the direction of Crossbarry. Majors Halahan and Percival moved towards the spot; they found that lorries, coming out to bring the troops home, had been ambushed by rebels, who, fortunately for themselves, had been lying out in ambush beside the road instead of in their bivouacs, on the off chance of some military lorry passing. Major Percival reached the spot first, with five men. He found the men in the act of setting the lorries on fire. He took up position and drove them off, but during the action one of his men was killed. Meantime, Major Halahan, with his men, attacked the position on the hills, driving back the rebels who held it; during this encounter, unfortunately, Lieut. Hotblack was killed when courageously leading his men. As to the convoy, the drivers of the leading lorries were killed and 2nd Lieut. Tower badly wounded in the chin. The hindermost lorry but one, managed to back out, and some of the wounded were picked up. Lieut. Tower, scratching instructions with a nail on the wall, retired with the party from that lorry and took up a position at a neighbouring farm. In this action eight men, including A.S.C. drivers, were killed. Sergeant Watts was missing; his body was subsequently found lying beside a heap of cartridges, showing that he had carried his Lewis gun forward in his endeavour to save the situation. His head had been smashed in, apparently with the butt-end of a rifle, after death. Although the encounter took such an unfortunate turn, the rebels doubtless suffered heavily. They never again faced the Essex men in the field.

INCIDENTS AND THE TRUCE.

Other stories were told in the barracks at Kinsale, which may here be added. Two unarmed soldiers were one day walking in Bandon, in a street in the town itself; they were "carried off and murdered in cold blood." A couple of naval men, attached to wireless, were taken at the same time; but these, after being questioned, were released. Almost simultaneously, one of the Essex was shot dead when walking in Courtmacksherry, from which place the detachment then at Timoleague had been taken. On another occasion, at a football match, a singular affray took place. The detachment at Bandon were playing the R.I.C., and during the game some rebels opened fire on the spectators. Corporal Seccombe, with a small escort, was present on the ground; he at once engaged these desperadoes and held them back while the troops retired to barracks. For this service he received the M.B.E.

During this period, too, much activity prevailed in places where notorious murders had been committed and where, in pursuance of official instructions for reprisals, houses were burned down. By July, 1921, two fresh regiments were brought into the area. These should have trebled the strength of the flying columns. The Government sanctioned the Truce when the troops were able to take the field in adequate numbers for the first time and when the morale of the Sinn Feiners was at its lowest, and many were suffering from scabies. Through all this hazardous, trying time, the whole battalion behaved admirably, although so many were hardly more than boys. We in England, I was assured, can with difficulty realize the strain caused by guerilla warfare of such a nature; month after month the men enjoyed but three nights in bed each week. Up to their leaving Kinsale, the casualties of the battalion totalled four officers and about 40 other ranks.

A SOUTHENDER'S STORY.

The foregoing, I think, will convey a fair impression of the work entailed on the battalion in South Ireland. It chanced, however, that I crossed the great barrack square to the Sergeants' Mess, and there, to an accompanying hubbub of talk, tea was being enjoyed for the last time at Kinsale. I had a chat with Sergeant A. E. Cooper, whose home is at 50, Leigh Road, Westcliff. He told me a short story illustrative of the battalion's recent "offensives," which, at the risk of repetition, I must tell in his own words, merely premising that he had received the *Southend Standard* weekly since arriving at Kinsale, and was evidently as pleased as I that two Southenders, in these strange, perilous days, should have met so far from home.

"I have been," said he, "fifteen months with the regiment, here at Kinsale, whilst it carried out many difficult operations against the rebels. At first we worked under a big disadvantage, because the rebels knew every inch of the country, and could get away so quickly after ambushing any of our parties. One day, a large party of our fellows left the barracks here, before daylight. I went with them. We proceeded by motor convoy to a place some eight or ten miles off. From that point small parties were detailed to scour the country over a very wide area. We were to round up all suspected male persons. The job proved very hard owing to the limited number available for each party, and the rough nature of the country. I set off with one lot, and we began to search a number of houses, instructions having been given as to what methods we were to adopt. We went in this way into several farms and cottages, arresting all male members of the families between 17 and 40 years old. Of course, the women in each house were very much upset, and this, naturally, made such jobs very distasteful. After about a couple of hours' work I had a large number of civilian prisoners in my charge, with only a small escort to look after them; some of these were youngsters quite unused to such work. In almost each instance these people gave themselves up without the least fuss or struggle—in fact, during all the time they were in my charge they never showed any signs of resistance.

"After completing this job, I took my prisoners to the appointed rendezvous. Here I met other parties, also with prisoners, and handed mine over to the senior officer. He lined them up on the roadside and questioned each. If a man seemed loyally disposed, and could give a reasonable account of himself he was allowed to make the best of his way home, and jolly well did so! If, on the other hand, he proved a strange or suspicious character, or showed signs of sympathy with the rebels, he was kept under close arrest, taken to the barracks, and there confined, to be put through a searching cross-examination by the Intellieco officer. Later in the day, all the search parties got together and returned to barracks by motor convoy. One of the lorries broke down, and a party was detailed for protective purposes. Nobody got much rest during this time, as other parties had to be made up for different work, to be carried out next day. I myself, after this, spent most of my time in the Q.M.'s office, and, therefore, took no active part in the work undertaken against the rebels, continued in April, May and June."

LAST HOURS.

That evening, at supper, I learned that other troops in South Ireland were the Hants. (already mentioned), the South Staffordshires, the Green Howards, and the Welsh Fusiliers. Sport, despite all hindrances, had not been neglected; inter-company hockey and football were contested; the miniature range became an improvized concert hall; boxing was enjoyed (especially by spectators), but three belts, presented to the regiment by Colonel Moffitt, were not "fought off" for lack of opportunity. The barracks, that night, would be given over, I was told, to Sinn Feiners and other "free" men; this, to be sure, was not palatable to the battalion. By this time almost everything lay at the railway station, awaiting entrainment; but a residue, living and dead, had yet to be transported thither. So I arose from the festive board and looked about me—in the dark quadrangle, in half deserted blocks, in the mess rooms.

Mules and horses, 26 in all, were promptly to be boxed, including "Whiteface," reputed, not without reason, to be "some horse." She was ridden by the Colonel, was at least 17 years old, and still going strong. "Whiteface" went to France with the "Pompadours" in 1914, took part in the retreat, and there stayed throughout the Great War. With the horses and mules, went smaller animals—all, in some sense, battalion mascots. There was "Nigger," a black Irish terrier; his usual residence had been Charles Fort. He proved himself a wily, sagacious brute, and should have been with the Roundhead searchers at Worcester, for once he spotted a Sinn Feiner hidden in a tree, whom no other eye had detected. He has a friend in the Drums, with whom he wages internecine strife. The drum's dog is able to count up to five, as if five pennies are given him and one taken away he carries out an exhaustive search for the missing coin. Then, I found, five cats were to share the evacuation, and to be introduced at Carrickfergus. All were descended from a common, sandyish progenitor, who came upstairs, after supper, for a last glance round. In addition there were three ferrets, for whose convenient transport to Ulster a box, well barred, was constructed under my eyes (and ears) in the Sergeant's Mess Last, but assuredly not least, I was privileged, in a room aloft, to see the drums—the four far-famed silver drums bearing the names of the regiment's battles in many lands. They are inscribed: "Presented by the County of Essex to the 1st Battalion, Essex Regiment, in recognition of distinguished services; 1913." The battalion has thirty silver bugles, but these I did not see, and two other most interesting drums, formed by cutting in half a very large one, captured from the Sinn Feiners. With the above, went that night an astonishing variety of musical and unmusical instruments belonging to the boys, and most dearly cherished. I may add a hint whispered in my ear by a little bird. The County of Essex, desiring to recognize the services of the 1st Battalion in Ireland, when all is over and piping times of peace are with us again, might do worse than present that most deserving unit with four more silver drums. What was it the bird added?

When once again in peace men meet,
Those silver drums should surely beat;
Announcing loud to all around
That gratitude on earth is found.

"THE LAST PHASE."

"The "Last Post" sounded at 10 o'cock. Soon after," "There was no small stir among the soldiers"; some 300 officers and men were to leave Kinsale by the 11.30 train, and a like number an hour later, completing the evacuation. Dr. Johnson, and after him De Quincey, wrote that men never do anything for the last time without sadness of heart. I am like Mr. Herbert Paul; "I venture to dispute this proposition." The sentry, looking into the darkness that brooded over Kinsale during his last hour on the bridge did so, I will answer for it, with no small satisfaction. The men, foregathering on the station platform, cast no "longing, lingering look behind." It is usually pleasant to turn the page, and I have yet to learn that life at Kinsale and its district had been congenial. Civil wars are all wars the worst; and as such the struggle in Ireland must be described.

I was to leave by the train next to start, so followed to the platform. Again a few Kinsale girls gathered to witness the last scenes, despite the lateness of the hour and the increasing violence of the elements. The rear-half of the train had already been backed and was in part loaded; horse-boxes were occupied, as plunging feet and stranger sounds betokened; limber wagons came next, well laden; carriages for officers and men were to be in front, the train extending far beyond the platform. Officers and sergeants moved briskly amongst the throng of other ranks, giving orders; gradually, what seemed a patterned configuration took shape, displacing the previous medley; the boys, from time to time, broke into little snatches of song as they awaited the order to entrain. In the waiting room a large fire burned brightly, throwing strange shadows to and fro across the farther wall; a private, seated near by, was warming tea in a large pail, at perilous balance on the live coals. Meantime, the girls ventured farther and farther along the platform; such liberties were for a while winked at, but as the moment of departure drew near, they were ordered off, obeying very slowly, not without show of grief.

Wind and rain had been busy all this time, and, now, as if to hurl imprecations at departing heads, the rains descended and the floods came. Gusts swept the platform with ever increasing violence; slanting rains beat pitilessly upon us all, the platform roof being far behind the passenger carriages, which did not arrive until long after the rear boxes and wagons. Sheets of water arose before the wind and were blown into stinging spray; blue lightning, of dazzling brightness, played intermittently across the sky, north and west; from the direction of Cork came more casual mutterings of thunder. Never, since the gentleman in "Lear" talked of "the to-and-fro-conflicting wind and rain," can much worse a night have fallen even upon old Ireland. But all entrained at last, and cheers—heard even above the uproar of nature—were raised as we drew away from Kinsale—"The Head of the Sea."

The following officers evacuated Kinsale with the N.C.O.'s and men that day, in addition to Lieut.-Col. Moffitt. I give their names in the order in which they were written down for me by a sergeant-major: Major R. Neave, Major R. N. Thompson, Major J. H. Pattison, D.S.O., Captain A. H. Blest, Lieut. F. A. S. Clarke, D.S.O., Lieut. N. R. Upton, M.B.E., Lieut. L. A. G. Bowen, M.C., Lieut. T. E. Fry, Lieut. H. J. W. Silver, M.C., Lieut. H. Alp; also 2nd-Lieut. J. W. K. E. Phelps, Captain and Quartermaster F. Richardson, Lieut. J. H. Phillips, R.F.A., and Captain R. B. Bryan, R.A.M.C.

RISKING IT.

The train crawled slowly away from Kinsale; I will own that when a mile distant therefrom I breathed more freely. I am, I hope, no alarmist, but I had heard more in Ireland than I can well repeat; I should have felt small surprise if, when we were once actually on the move, shots had been fired in the darkness at the passing train. That very day a train bound for Dublin was ambushed; moreover, to my mind, the utter silence in the district as the troops came together was suspicious; those girls alone, so far as I saw, represented the inhabitants when the soldiers left. But nothing happened; Kinsale Junction—some miles from the town—was safely passed, and in due time we drew towards Bandon station in West Cork. Somewhere in Cork I must needs alight, but it was by no means certain where the train would stop. I might be carried on far beyond the city if, perforce, the journey was continued without a break; if, on the other hand, I got down alone at any point where we pulled up, I might expect, as the observed of all observers, to be asked my business, which might all too sufficiently be gathered from my notebook. It seemed difficult to avoid both horns of this dilemma; I was much tumbled in mind, yet hoping for the best, when, with a jerk, the train drew up some 400 yards from the station. It might be then or never. I got out upon the footboard, jumped to the ground, and walked beside the metals towards the station. I was hailed from the open window of a signal box as I picked my way across points and over sleepers, but took no notice. The station platform was deserted, but at the far end, beyond the exit, five men stood together, watching my approach. But kindly Providence had ordered that one of that five should be a ticket inspector; to him I explained the situation, and, on hearing that I had travelled on the troop train by permission of the O.C., he became positively kindly, accepted my fare, and, without looking at the four other men, I went out into the streets of Cork.

In Cork, the railroad from one station to the other runs across the thoroughfares, and the train from which I had descended presently clattered past. It was by this nearly 1 o'clock; what sounded like shuntings came to me from the direction of the farther station, and whether or no the train stopped at Cork or ran straight through, I have yet to learn. There, anyway, rough scenes had quite recently been witnessed on the departure of troops. Girls, it seems, gathered with other folk to see the soldiers embark or entrain — I forget which — and some show of regret on their part aroused the ire of watchful ruffians. The girls were harshly handled; were even struck on the head and about the body with heavy sticks; one, more cruelly cut than the rest, bled to death. Incidentally, I may mention that other girls guilty only of showing friendliness towards English troops, have had their hair cut close to the head.

CARRICKFERGUS.

The town towards which the battalion rode that night is, as readers may know, a maritime one, in the province of Ulster. The two towns, Kinsale and Carrickfergus, come singularly together in Irish history; for at Kinsale James II., as I have said, landed when endeavouring to regain a lost crown and kingdom, whilst his supplanter, William III., landed at Carrickfergus to frustrate that effort. The town is some ten miles from Belfast, recent figures relative to its religious complexion are not to my hand; fifty years back, I read, the Protestants and Catholics were as seven to one. It was the scene of the first Presbytery ever held in Ireland; Scotch Covenanters, in the reign of Charles I., found it a safe refuge from the persecutor; in 1760, strange to relate, it was captured, and held for a few days, by a French squadron led by Commodore Thourot. To-day Carrickfergus is near the core and centre of Ireland's worst troubles, and the Essex Regiment may see lively service in the neighbourhood. Even apart from its share in the Great War, it has a high reputation to maintain. It will maintain it to the full.

SIDELIGHTS.

The train from Cork to Rosslare, connecting with the boat for Fishguard, runs on Wednesday evenings, so I had many hours in which to kick my heels in Cork. I wrote a little from rough notes, walked in the higher quarter of the city, overlooking the quays, but saw little through the almost continuous veils of mist, rain or snow. Now and then I talked with my hostess—a Scotch lady who settled in the city many years ago, and is now mother-in-law to a Southend journalist. From her I learned many unpleasant details of the state of Ireland—that appalling subject upon which Spenser (who owned the Castle of Kilcolman and 3,000 acres in County Cork) found so much to write, more than three centuries ago. She told of the Black and Tans, who scared so many people by firing their revolvers in the air, for no obvious reasons, and who, when the mood took them, would enter an eating house, obtain all they needed, and walk out without paying a farthing—they did this, day after day, in many a town and village. From her I heard much of the "unknown destination," to which men obnoxious to Sinn Feiners were driven, and from which they did not return; also of the sinister means employed for the gathering of intelligence, and of many outrages which I need not narrate. An incident mentioned by her was, I thought, typical of the feeling that runs so high in the country. A man came to paint a lady's house—in particular the front door; "You ought to have it painted green," said he, "for you have been in Cork long enough to have become true Irish."

And so, on Wednesday evening, Feb. 22nd, I left Cork carrying with me many vivid impressions of my first visit to Ireland. Nothing short of the peculiar circumstances of the time and common usage would reconcile me to the word "rebel" as descriptive of any class of native Irishmen — for whose self-government I have spoken, written and voted—however extreme in views or strange in practices. A day is dawning when, we hope, the Ulster lion will lie down with the Sinn Fein lamb (readers can transfer the metaphor if they please); and when peace and goodwill, a "Union of Hearts" indeed, shall be found from the Giants' Causeway in farthest Ulster, to Skibbereen in County Cork, and England be respected in Ireland, and Ireland respected in England.

CONFIDENTIAL

WAR DIARY
OF
1ST BATTN.
THE ESSEX REGT
FOR
MARCH 1919.

VOL 49.

Army Form C. 2118.

WAR DIARY

Instructions regarding War Diaries and Intelligence Summaries are contained in F.S. Regs., Part II. and the Staff Manual respectively. Title pages will be prepared in manuscript.

(Erase heading not required.)

Place	Date MAR	Hour	Summary of Events and Information	Remarks and references to Appendices
RANSART	1		The Battⁿ was employed on Regimental Duties Gregg C.A.Wheat Divisional Race Meeting C.A. Gregg	
"	2		Church Parade C.A. Gregg	
"	3		The Battⁿ was employed on Regimental Duties C.A. Gregg	
"	4		" " " " " C.A. Gregg	
"	5		" " " " " C.A. Gregg	
"	6		Two officers:- Lieut. F.V. Smith and 2/Lieut L.J. Thompson and 58 O.R. were transferred to the 15th Battⁿ The Essex Regt C.A.Gregg	
"	7		The Battⁿ was employed on Regimental Duties C.A. Gregg	
"	8		" " " " " C.A. Gregg	
"	9		Church Parade C.A. Gregg	
"	10		The Battⁿ moved into the JUMET AREA C.A. Gregg	
JUMET	11		The Battⁿ was employed on Regimental Duties C.A. Gregg	

Army Form C. 2118.

WAR DIARY / INTELLIGENCE SUMMARY

(Erase heading not required.)

Place	Date	Hour	Summary of Events and Information	Remarks and references to Appendices
JUMET	MAR 12		Lt Col T.J.E. BIRKE, D.S.O. was discharged from Hospital + returned to the Battalion C.O. Gyngo	
"	13		The Battn was employed on Regimental Duties C.O. Gyngo	
"	14		Battn Kit Inspection – The Battn at H.Mf.F ST LOUIS, JUMET went allotted the Battalion from 0800 hrs to 1200 hrs C.O. Gyngo	
"	15		The Battn was employed on Regimental Duties C.O. Gyngo	
"	16		Battalion Church Parade C.O. Gyngo	
"	17		The Battn was employed on Regimental Duties C.O. Gyngo	
"	18		"	
"	19		"	
"	20		"	C.O. Gyngo
"	21		"	
"	22		"	
"	23		Battalion Church Parade	

Army Form C. 2118.

WAR DIARY / INTELLIGENCE SUMMARY

(Erase heading not required.)

Place	Date MAR	Hour	Summary of Events and Information	Remarks and references to Appendices
JUMET	24		FOOTBALL MATCH – 111TH BDE v 112TH BDE on the 10th R.F's Ground	C.Q.
"	25		The Battn. was employed on Regimental Duties	C.Q.
"	26		CAPT. G.A.M. PAXTON assumes command of the Battn. in the absence of LT. COL. T.J.E. BLAKE, D.S.O. on Leave	C.Q.
"	28		The Battn. was employed on Regimental Duties	C.Q.
"	29.		LT. COL. T.J.E. BLAKE, D.S.O. assumes command of the battalion from today.	C.Q.
"	30		Church Parade	C.Q.
"	31		The Battalion was employed on Regimental Duties	C.Q.

Terence Blake
Lt Col
Cmdg 1st East R. Rif.

RETURN shewing decrease in strength for the month of

Strength of Unit, 1ST MARCH 1919 — 27 Off   291 ORs | OFF | OR |
                                                             | 27 | 291 |

Decrease during month:- | OFF | O.R. |
(a) Demobilized:- | 1 | 70 |
    Coalminers   --------
    Pivotals   ---------
    Long Service -------- | OFF | O.R. |
    Watford Details -- | 1 | 70 |
    etc.   etc.

(b) Evacuated sick and struck --- | 2 | 5 |
    off strength

(c) Other causes Transfer to A of Occ' | 2 | 119 | 5 | 194 |

Strength of Unit, 1ST APRIL 1919. ---------------------   22 | 97 |

J.H. Mackay Paxton Capt & Lt Col
Comdg 1ST Bn The Essex Rgt.

2-4-19.

www.ingramcontent.com/pod-product-compliance
Lightning Source LLC
Chambersburg PA
CBHW081540160426
43191CB00011B/1799